ROOTABAGA
• PIGEONS •

BY
CARL SANDBURG

Author of "Rootabaga Stories," "Slabs of the Sunburnt West,"
"Smoke and Steel," "Chicago Poems," "Cornhuskers"

ILLUSTRATIONS AND DECORATIONS
BY
MAUD AND MISKA PETERSHAM

D1552477

APPLEWOOD BOOKS
BEDFORD, MASSACHUSETTS

Rootabaga Pigeons was originally published by Harcourt, Brace and Company, Inc., in 1923.

ISBN 978-1-55709-509-1

Thank you for purchasing an Applewood Book.
Applewood reprints America's lively classics—books from the past that are still of interest to modern readers. For a free copy of our current catalog, write to:
Applewood Books, P.O. Box 365, Bedford, MA 01730.

Library of Congress Card Number: 00-110612

To Three Illinois Pigeons

CONTENTS

1.

Two Stories Told by the Potato Face Blind Man

2.

Two Stories About Bugs and Eggs

3.

Five Stories About Hatrack the Horse, Six Pigeons, Three Wild Babylonian Baboons, Six Umbrellas, Bozo the Button Buster

Contents

Contents

FULL-PAGE ILLUSTRATIONS

1. Two Stories Told by the Potato Face Blind Man.

People: Blixie Bimber
Blixie Bimber's Mother
The Potato Face Blind Man
A Green Rat with the Rheumatism
Bricklayers
Mortar Men
Riveters
A Skyscraper

Slipfoot
A Stairway to the Moon
A Trapeze

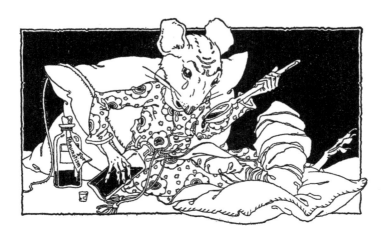

The Skyscraper to the Moon and How the Green Rat with the Rheumatism Ran a Thousand Miles Twice

Blixie Bimber's mother was chopping hash. And the hatchet broke. So Blixie started downtown with fifteen cents to buy a new hash hatchet for chopping hash.

Downtown she peeped around the corner next nearest the postoffice where the Potato Face Blind Man sat with his accordion. And the old man had his legs crossed, one foot on the sidewalk, the other foot up in the air.

The foot up in the air had a green rat sitting on it, tying the old man's shoestrings in knots and double knots. Whenever the old man's foot wiggled and wriggled the green rat wiggled and wriggled.

The tail of the rat wrapped five wraps around the shoe and then fastened and tied like a package.

On the back of the green rat was a long white swipe from the end of the nose to the end of the tail. Two little white swipes stuck up over the eyelashes. And five short thick swipes of white played pussy-wants-a-corner back of the ears and along the ribs of the green rat.

They were talking, the old man and the green rat, talking about alligators and why the alligators keep their baby shoes locked up in trunks over the winter time—and why the rats in the moon lock their mittens in ice boxes.

"I had the rheumatism last summer a year

ago," said the rat. "I had the rheumatism so bad I ran a thousand miles south and west till I came to the Egg Towns and stopped in the Village of Eggs Up."

"So?" quizzed the Potato Face.

"There in the Village of Eggs Up, they asked me, 'Do you know how to stop the moon moving?' I answered them, 'Yes, I know how—a baby alligator told me—but I told the baby alligator I wouldn't tell.'

"Many years ago there in that Village of Eggs Up they started making a skyscraper to go up till it reached the moon. They said, 'We will step in the elevator and go up to the roof and sit on the roof and eat supper on the moon.'

"The bricklayers and the mortar men and the iron riveters and the wheelbarrowers and the plasterers went higher and higher making that skyscraper, till at last they were half way up to the moon, saying to each other while they worked, 'We will step in the elevator and go up to the roof and sit on the roof and eat supper on the moon.'

"Yes, they were halfway up to the moon. And that night looking at the moon they saw it move and they said to each other, 'We must stop the moon moving,' and they said later, 'We don't know how to stop the moon moving.'

"And the bricklayers and the mortar men and the iron riveters and the wheelbarrowers and the plasterers said to each other, 'If we go on now and make this skyscraper it will miss the moon and we will never go up in the elevator and sit on the roof and eat supper on the moon.'

"So they took the skyscraper down and started making it over again, aiming it straight at the moon again. And one night standing looking at the moon they saw it move and they said to each other, 'We must stop the moon moving,' saying later to each other, 'We don't know how to stop the moon moving.'

The Green Rat with Rheumatism

"And now they stand in the streets at night there in the Village of Eggs Up, stretching their necks looking at the moon, and asking each other, 'Why does the moon move and how can we stop the moon moving?'

"Whenever I saw them standing there stretching their necks looking at the moon, I had a zig-zag ache in my left hind foot and I wanted to tell them what the baby alligator told me, the secret of how to stop the moon moving. One night that ache zig-zagged me so—way inside my left hind foot—it zig-zagged so I ran home here a thousand miles."

The Potato Face Blind Man wriggled his shoe—and the green rat wriggled—and the long white swipe from the end of the nose to the end of the tail of the green rat wriggled.

"Is your rheumatism better?" the old man asked.

The rat answered, "Any rheumatism is better if you run a thousand miles twice."

The Skyscraper to the Moon

And Blixie Bimber going home with the fifteen cent hash hatchet for her mother to chop hash, Blixie said to herself, "It is a large morning to be thoughtful about."

Slipfoot and How He Nearly Always Never Gets What He Goes After

Blixie Bimber flipped out of the kitchen one morning, first saying good-by to the dish-pan, good-by to the dish-rag, good-by to the dish-towel for wiping dishes.

Under one arm she put a basket of peonies she picked, under the other arm she put a basket of jonquils she picked.

Then she flipped away up the street and downtown where she put the baskets of peonies and jonquils one on each side of the Potato Face Blind Man.

"I picked the pink and lavender peonies and I picked the yellow jonquils for you to be smelling one on each side of you this fine early summer morning," she said to the Potato Face. "Have you seen anybody good to see lately?"

"Slipfoot was here this morning," said the old man.

"And who is Slipfoot?" asked Blixie.

"I don't know. He says to me, 'I got a foot always slips. I used to wash windows—and my foot slips. I used to be king of the collar buttons, king of a million dollars—and my foot slips. I used to be king of the peanuts, king of a million dollars again. I used to be king of the oyster cans, selling a million cans a day. I used to be king of the peanut sacks, selling ten million sacks a day. And every time I was a king my foot slips. Every time I had a million dollars my foot slips. Every

On the last step of the stairway my foot slips

time I went high and put my foot higher my foot slips. Somebody gave me a slipfoot. I always slip.' "

"So you call him Slipfoot?" asked Blixie.

"Yes," said the old man.

"Has he been here before?"

"Yes, he was here a year ago, saying, 'I marry a woman and she runs away. I run after her—and my foot slips. I always get what I want—and then my foot slips.

"I ran up a stairway to the moon one night. I shoveled a big sack full of little gold beans, little gold bricks, little gold bugs, on the moon and I ran down the stairway from the moon. On the last step of the stairway, my foot slips —and all the little gold beans, all the little gold bricks, all the little gold bugs, spill out and spill away. When I get down the stairway I am holding the sack and the sack holds nothing. I am all right always till my foot slips.

"I jump on a trapeze and I go swinging,

13

swinging, swinging out where I am going to take hold of the rainbow and bring it down where we can look at it close. And I hang by my feet on the trapeze and I am swinging out where I am just ready to take hold of the rainbow and bring it down. Then my foot slips."

"What is the matter with Slipfoot?" asks Blixie.

"He asks me that same question," answered the Potato Face Blind Man. "He asks me that every time he comes here. I tell him all he needs is to get his slipfoot fixed so it won't slip. Then he'll be all right."

"I understand you," said Blixie. "You make it easy. You always make it easy. And before I run away will you promise me to smell of the pink and lavender peonies and the yellow jonquils all day to-day?"

"I promise," said the Potato Face. "Promises are easy. I like promises."

"So do I," said the little girl. "It's prom-

14

ises pushing me back home to the dish-pan, the dish-rag, and the dish-towel for wiping dishes."

"Look out you don't get a slipfoot," warned the old man as the girl flipped up the street going home.

2. Two Stories About Bugs and Eggs.

People: Little Bugs
Big Bugs
The Rag Doll
The Broom Handle
Hammer and Nails
The Hot Cookie Pan
The Ice Tongs
The Coal Bucket
The Bushel Basket
Jack Knife
Kindling Wood
Splinters

Shush Shush
The Postmaster
The Hardware Man
The Policeman
The Postmaster's Hat
A Buff Banty Egg

Many, Many Weddings in One Corner House

There was a corner house with corners every way it looked. And up in the corners were bugs with little bug houses, bug doors to open, bug windows to look out of.

In the summer time if the evening was cool or in the winter time if the evening was warm, they played games—bugs-up, bugs-down, run-bugs-run, beans-bugs-beans.

This corner house was the place the Rag

Many, Many Weddings

Doll and the Broom Handle came to after their wedding. This was the same time those old people, Hammer and Nails, moved into the corner house with all the little Hammers and all the little Nails.

So there they were, the young couple, the Rag Doll and the Broom Handle, and that old family, Hammer and Nails, and up in the corners among the eave troughs and the roof shingles, the bugs with little bug houses, bug doors to open, bug windows to look out of, and bug games—bugs-up, bugs-down, run-bugs-run, or beans-bugs-beans.

Around the corner of the house every Saturday morning came the Hot Cookie Pan with a pan of hot cookies for Sunday, Monday, Tuesday, Wednesday and the rest of the week.

The Ice Tongs came with ice, the Coal Bucket came with coal, the Potato Sack came with potatoes. And the Bushel Basket was always going or coming and saying under his breath, "*Bushels, bushels, bushels.*"

The Hot Cookie Pan came with a pan of hot cookies
and the Coal Bucket with coal

In One Corner House

One day the bugs in the little bug houses opened the bug doors and looked out of the bug windows and said to each other, "They are washing their shirts and sewing on buttons— there is going to be a wedding."

And the next day the bugs said, "They are going to have a wedding and a wedding breakfast for Jack Knife and Kindling Wood. They are asking everybody in the kitchen, the cellar, and the back yard, to come."

The wedding day came. The people came. From all over the kitchen, the cellar, the back yard, they came. The Rag Doll and the Broom Handle were there. Hammer and Nails and all the little Hammers and all the little Nails were there. The Ice Tongs, the Coal Bucket, the Potato Sack, were all there —and the Bushel Basket going and coming and saying under his breath, *"Bushels, bushels, bushels."* And, of course, the Hot Cookie Pan was there hopping up and down with hot cookies.

Many, Many Weddings

So Jack Knife and Kindling Wood began living in the corner house. A child came. They named her Splinters. And the Hot Cookie Pan and Splinters met and kissed each other and sat together in cozy corners close to each other.

And the bugs high up in the corners in the little bug houses, they opened the bug doors, looked out of the bug windows and said, "They are washing their shirts and sewing on buttons, there is a wedding again—the Hot Cookie Pan and Splinters."

And now they have many, many children, the Hot Cookie Pan and Splinters. Their children have gone all over the world and everybody knows them.

"Whenever you find a splinter or a sliver or a shiny little shaving of wood in a hot cookie," the bugs in the little bug houses say, "whenever you find a splinter or a sliver or a shiny little shaving of wood in a hot cookie, it is the child of the Hot Cookie Pan and the girl named Splinters, the daughter of Jack Knife and Kindling Wood, who grew up and married the Hot Cookie Pan."

And sometimes if a little bug asks a big bug a queer, quivvical, quizzical question hard to answer, the big bug opens a bug door, looks out of a bug window and says to the little bug, "If you don't believe what we tell you, go and ask Hammer and Nails or any of the little Hammers and Nails. Then run and listen to the Bushel Basket going and coming and saying under his breath, *'Bushels, bushels, bushels.'* "

Shush Shush, the Big Buff Banty Hen Who Laid an Egg in the Postmaster's Hat

Shush Shush was a big buff banty hen. She lived in a coop. Sometimes she marched out of the coop and went away and.laid eggs. But always she came back to the coop.

And whenever she went to the front door and laid an egg in the door-bell, she rang the bell once for one egg, twice for two eggs, and a dozen rings for a dozen eggs.

Once Shush Shush went into the house of the Sniggers family and laid an egg in the piano. Another time she climbed up in the clock and laid an egg in the clock. But always she came back to the coop.

One summer morning Shush Shush marched out through the front gate, up to the next corner and the next, till she came to the post-office. There she walked into the office of the postmaster and laid an egg in the postmaster's hat.

The postmaster put on his hat, went to the hardware store and bought a keg of nails. He took off his hat and the egg dropped into the keg of nails.

The hardware man picked up the egg, put it in *his* hat, and went out to speak to a police-man. He took off his hat, speaking to the policeman, and the egg dropped on the side-walk.

The policeman picked up the egg and put

it in *his* police hat. The postmaster came past; the policeman took off his police hat and the egg dropped down on the sidewalk.

The postmaster said, "I lost that egg, it is my egg," picked it up, put it in his postmaster's hat, and forgot all about having an egg in his hat.

Then the postmaster, a long tall man, came to the door of the postoffice, a short small door. And the postmaster didn't stoop low, didn't bend under, so he bumped his hat and his head on the top of the doorway. And the egg *broke* and ran down over his face and neck.

And long before that happened, Shush Shush was home in her coop, standing in the door saying, "It is a big day for me because I laid one of my big buff banty eggs in the postmaster's hat."

There Shush Shush stays, living in a coop. Sometimes she marches out of the coop and goes away and lays eggs in pianos, clocks,

Shush, Shush, the Big Buff Banty Hen

hats.   But she always comes back to the coop.

And whenever she goes to the front door and lays an egg in the door-bell, she rings the bell once for one egg, twice for two eggs, and a dozen rings for a dozen eggs.

3. Five Stories About Hatrack the
   Horse, Six Pigeons, Three Wild
   Babylonian Baboons, Six Umbrel-
   las, Bozo the Button Buster.

People: Hatrack the Horse
Peter Potato Blossom Wishes
Rag Bag Mammy
Gimmes

Wiffle the Chick
Chickamauga
Chattanooga
Chattahoochee
Blue Mist
Bubbles
Wednesday Evening in the
    Twilight and the Gloaming
Telegrams

The Three Wild Babylonian
    Baboons
Three Umbrellas
The Night Policeman

Six Umbrellas
The Big Umbrella
Straw Hats
Dippy the Wisp

Bozo the Button Buster
A Mouse
Deep Red Roses
The Beans Are Burning
Sweeter Than the Bees Hum-
    ming

How Rag Bag Mammy Kept Her Secret While the Wind Blew Away the Village of Hat Pins

There was a horse-face man in the Village of Cream Puffs. People called him Hatrack the Horse.

The skin stretched tight over his bones. Once a little girl said, "His eyes look like lightning bugs lighting up the summer night coming out of two little doors."

When Hatrack the Horse took *off* his hat he reached his hand around behind and hung the hat *on* a shoulder bone sticking out.

33

When he wanted to put *on* his hat he reached his hand around and took it *off* from where it was hanging on the shoulder bone sticking out behind.

One summer Hatrack said to Peter Potato Blossom Wishes, "I am going away up north and west in the Rootabaga Country to see the towns different from each other. Then I will come back east as far as I went west, and south as far as I went north, till I am back again where my little pal, Peter Potato Blossom Wishes, lives in the Village of Cream Puffs."

So he went away, going north and west and coming back east and south till he was back again in his home town, sitting on the front steps of his little red shanty, fixing a kite to fly.

"Are you glad to come back?" asked Peter.

"Yes, this is home, this is the only place where I know how the winds act up so I can talk to them when I fly a kite."

"Tell me what you saw and how you listened

and if they handed you any nice packages."

"They handed me packages, all right, all right," said Hatrack the Horse.

"Away far to the west I came to the Village of Hat Pins," he went on. "It is the place where they make all the hat pins for the hats to be pinned on in the Rootabaga Country. They asked me about the Village of Cream Puffs and how the winds are here because the winds here blow so many hats off that the Village of Hat Pins sells more hat pins to the people here than anywhere else.

"There is an old woman in the Village of Hat Pins. She walks across the town and around the town every morning and every afternoon. On her back is a big rag bag. She never takes anything out of the rag bag. She never puts anything in. That is, nobody ever sees her put anything in or take anything out. She has never opened the rag bag telling people to take a look and see what is in it. She sleeps

35

with the rag bag for a pillow. So it is always with her and nobody looks into it unless she lets them. And she never lets them.

"Her name? Everybody calls her Rag Bag Mammy. She wears aprons with big pockets. And though she never speaks to big grown-up people she is always glad to meet little growing people, boys and girls. And especially, most of all, she likes to meet boys and girls who say, 'Gimme' (once, like that) or 'Gimme, gimme' (twice, like that) or 'Gimme, gimme, gimme' (three times) or 'Gimme, gimme, gimme, gimme, gimme, gimme' (more times than we can count). She likes to meet the gimmes because she digs into her pockets and brings out square chocolate drops and round chocolate drops and chocolate drops shaped like a half moon, barber pole candy with red and white stripes wrapped around it, all day suckers so long they last not only all day but all this week and all next week, and different kinds of jack-stones, some that say chink-chink on the sidewalks and some that say teentsy-weentsy chink-chink when they all bunch together on the sidewalk. And sometimes if one of the gimmes is crying and feeling bad she gives the gimme a doll only as big as a child's hand but the doll can say the alphabet and sing little Chinese Assyrian songs.

"Of course," said Hatrack the Horse, reaching his hand around to see if his hat was hanging on behind, "of course, you have to have sharp ears and listen close-up and be nice when you are listening, if you are going to hear a doll say the alphabet and sing little Chinese Assyrian songs."

"I could hear them," said Peter Potato Blossom Wishes. "I am a nice listener. I could hear those dolls sing the little Chinese Assyrian songs."

"I believe you, little pal of mine," said Hatrack. "I know you have the ears and you know how to put your ears so you hear."

"Of course, every morning and every afternoon when Rag Bag Mammy walks across the town and around the town in the Village of Hat Pins, people ask her what is in the rag bag on her back. And she answers, 'It is a nice day we are having,' or 'I think the rain will stop when it stops raining, don't you?' Then if they ask again and beg and plead, '*What* is in the rag bag? What *is* in the rag bag?' she tells them, 'When the wind blows away the Village of Hat Pins and blows it so far away it never comes back, then—then, then, then— I will tell you what is in the rag bag.' "

"One day the wind came along and blew the Village of Hat Pins loose, and after blowing it loose, carried it high off in the sky. And the people were saying to each other, 'Well, now we are going to hear Rag Bag Mammy tell us what is in the rag bag.'

"And the wind kept blowing, carrying the Village of Hat Pins higher and farther and farther and higher. And when at last it went away so high it came to a white cloud, the hat pins in the village all stuck out and fastened the village to the cloud so the wind couldn't blow it any farther.

"And—after a while they pulled the hat-pins out of the cloud—and the village dropped back right down where it was before.

"And Rag Bag Mammy goes every morning and every afternoon with the rag bag on her back across and around the town. And sometimes people say to her, 'The next time the wind blows us away—the next time the wind will blow us so far there won't be any cloud to fasten hat pins in—and you will have to tell us what is in the rag bag.' And Rag Bag Mammy just answers, 'Yes, yes—yes— yes,' and goes on her way looking for the next boy or girl to say, 'Gimme' (once, like that) or 'Gimme, gimme' (twice, like that) or 'Gimme, gimme, gimme, gimme, gimme' (more times than we can count).

"And if a child is crying she digs into her pockets and pulls out the doll that says the alphabet and sings little Chinese Assyrian songs."

"And," said Peter Potato Blossom Wishes, "you have to listen close up with your ears and be nice when you are listening."

"In the Village of Hat Pins that the wind nearly blew away forever," said Hatrack the Horse.

And Peter Potato Blossom Wishes skipped away down from the little red shanty, skipped down the street, and then began walking slow saying to herself, "I love Hatrack the Horse like a grand uncle—his eyes look like lightning bugs lighting up the summer night coming out of two little doors."

How Six Pigeons Came Back to Hatrack the Horse After Many Accidents and Six Telegrams

Six crooked ladders stood against the front of the shanty where Hatrack the Horse lived.

Yellow roses all on fire were climbing up and down the ladders, up and down and crossways.

And leaning out on both sides from the crooked ladders were vines of yellow roses, leaning, curving, nearly falling.

Hatrack the Horse was waiting. This was the morning Wiffle the Chick was coming.

41

How Six Pigeons Came Back

"Sit here on the cracker box and listen," he said to her when she came; "listen and you will hear the roses saying, 'This is climbing time for all yellow roses and climbing time is the time to climb; how did we ever learn to climb only by climbing?   Listen and you will hear—st. .th. .st. .th. .st. .th. .it is the feet of the yellow roses climbing up and down and leaning out and curving and nearly falling .st. .th. .st. .th. .' "

So Wiffle the Chick sat there, early in the summer, enjoying herself, sitting on a cracker box, listening to the yellow roses climb around the six crooked ladders.

Hatrack the Horse came out.   On his shoulders were two pigeons, on his hands two pigeons.   And he reached his hand around behind his back where his hat was hanging and he opened the hat and showed Wiffle the Chick two pigeons in the hat.

"They are lovely pigeons to look at and their

To Hatrack the Horse

eyes are full of lessons to learn," said Wiffle the Chick. "Maybe you will tell me why you have their feet wrapped in bandages, hospital liniment bandages full of hospital liniment smells? Why do you put soft mittens on the feet of these pigeons so lovely to look at?"

"They came back yesterday, they came back home," was the answer. "They came back limping on their feet with the toes turned in so far they nearly turned backward. When they put their bleeding feet in my hands one by one each one, it was like each one was writing his name in my hand with red ink."

"Did you know they were coming?" asked Wiffle.

"Every day the last six days I get a telegram, six telegrams from six pigeons—and at last they come home. And ever since they come home they are telling me they come because they love Hatrack the Horse and the yellow climbing roses climbing over the six crooked ladders."

43

How Six Pigeons Came Back

"Did you name your pigeons with names?" asked Wiffle.

"These three, the sandy and golden brown, all named themselves by where they came from. This is Chickamauga, here is Chattanooga, and this is Chattahoochee. And the other three all got their names from me when I was feeling high and easy. This is Blue Mist, here is Bubbles, and last of all take a look at Wednesday Evening in the Twilight and the Gloaming."

"Do you always call her Wednesday Evening in the Twilight and the Gloaming?"

"Not when I am making coffee for breakfast. If I am making coffee for breakfast then I just call her Wednesday Evening."

"Didn't you tie the mittens on her feet extra special nice?"

"Yes—she is an extra special nice pigeon. She cries for pity when she wants pity. And she shuts her eyes when she doesn't want to look at you. And if you look deep in her eyes

44

when her eyes are open you will see lights there exactly like the lights on the pastures and the meadows when the mist is drifting on a Wednesday evening just between the twilight and the gloaming.

"A week ago yesterday they all went away. And they won't tell why they went away. Somebody clipped their wings, cut off their flying feathers so they couldn't fly—and they won't tell why. They were six hundred miles from home—but they won't tell how they counted the six hundred miles. A hundred miles a lay they walked, six hundred miles in a week, and they sent a telegram to me every day, one writing a telegram one day and another writing a telegram the next day—all the time walking a hundred miles a day with their toes turned in like pigeon toes turn in. Do you wonder they needed bandages, hospital liniment bandages on their feet—and soft mittens?"

"Show me the telegrams they sent you, one

every day, for six days while they were walking six hundred miles on their pigeon toes."

So Hatrack the Horse got the six telegrams. The reading on the telegrams was like this:

1. "Feet are as good as wings if you have to. CHICKAMAUGA."

2. "If you love to go somewhere it is easy to walk. CHATTANOOGA."

3. "In the night sleeping you forget whether you have wings or feet or neither. CHATTAHOOCHEE."

4. "What are toes for if they don't point to what you want? BLUE MIST."

5. "Anybody can walk hundreds of miles putting one foot ahead of the other. BUBBLES."

6. "Pity me. Far is far. Near is near. And there is no place like home when the yellow roses climb up the ladders and sing in the early summer. Pity me. WEDNESDAY EVENING IN THE TWILIGHT AND THE GLOAMING."

46

To Hatrack the Horse

"Did they have any accidents going six hundred miles walking with their little pigeon toes turned in?" asked Wiffle.

"Once they had an accident," said Hatrack, with Chattahoochee standing in his hat, Chickamauga on his right shoulder, Chattanooga on his left, and holding Blue Mist and Bubbles on his wrists. "They came to an old wooden bridge. Chattahoochee and Wednesday Evening both cried out, 'The bridge will fall if we all walk on it the same time!' But they were all six already on the bridge and the bridge began sagging and tumbled them all into the river. But it was good for them all to have a footbath for their feet, Wednesday Evening explained."

"I got a suspicion you like Wednesday Evening in the Twilight and the Gloaming best of all," spoke up Wiffle.

"Well, Wednesday Evening was the only one I noticed making any mention of the yellow roses in her telegram," Hatrack the

How Six Pigeons Came Back

Horse explained, as he picked up Wednesday Evening and reached her around and put her to perch on the shoulder bone on his back.

Then the old man and the girl sat on the cracker box saying nothing, only listening to the yellow roses all on fire with early summer climbing up the crooked ladders, up and down and crossways, some of them leaning out and curving and nearly falling.

How the Three Wild Babylonian Baboons Went Away in the Rain Eating Bread and Butter

One morning when Hatrack the Horse went away from his shanty, he put three umbrellas in the corner next to the front door.

His pointing finger pointed at the three umbrellas as he said, "If the three wild Babylonian Baboons come sneaking up to this shanty and sneaking through the door and sneaking through the house, then all you three umbrellas open up like it was raining, jump straight at the baboons and fasten your handles in their hands. Then, all three of you stay open as if it was raining—and hold those handles in the hands of the baboons and never let go till I come."

Hatrack the Horse went away. The three umbrellas stood in the corner next to the front door. And when the umbrellas listened they could hear the three wild Babylonian Baboons sneaking up to the shanty. Soon the baboons, all hairy all over, bangs down their foreheads, came sneaking through the door. Just as they were sneaking through the door they took off their hats to show they were getting ready to sneak through the house.

Then the three umbrellas in the corner opened up as if it was raining; they jumped straight at the three wild Babylonian Baboons;

Away in Rain Eating Bread and Butter

and they fastened their handles tight in the hands of the baboons and wouldn't let go.

So there were the three wild Babylonian Baboons, each with a hat in his left hand, and an open umbrella in his right hand.

When Hatrack the Horse came home he came, quiet. He opened the front door, quiet. Then he looked around inside the house, quiet.

In the corner where he had stood the three umbrellas, he saw the three wild Babylonian Baboons on the floor, sleeping, with umbrellas over their faces.

"The umbrellas were so big they couldn't get through the door," said Hatrack the Horse. For a long time he stood looking at the bangs hanging down the foreheads of the baboons while they were sleeping. He took a comb and combed the bangs down the foreheads of the baboons. He went to the cupboard and spread bread and butter. He took the hats out of the left hands of the baboons and put the hats on their heads. He put a piece of bread and butter in the hand of each baboon.

After that he snipped each one across the nose with his finger (*snippety-snip!* just like that). They opened their eyes and stood up. Then he loosened the umbrella handles from their right hands and led them to the door.

They all looked out. It was raining. "Now you can go," he told the baboons. And they all walked out of the front door, and they seemed to be snickering and hiding the snickers.

The last he saw of them they were walking away in the rain eating bread and butter. And they took off their hats so the rain ran down and slid off on the bangs of their foreheads.

Hatrack the Horse turned to the umbrellas and said, "We know how to make a surprise party when we get a visit from the Babylonian

Away in Rain Eating Bread and Butter

Baboons with their bangs falling down their foreheads—don't we?"

That is what happened, as Hatrack the Horse told it to the night policeman in the Village of Cream Puffs.

How Six Umbrellas Took Off Their Straw Hats to Show Respect to the One Big Umbrella

Wherever Dippy the Wisp went she was always changing hats. She carried two hat boxes with big picture hats on her *right* arm. And she carried two hat boxes with big picture hats on her *left* arm. And she changed from green and gold hats to purple and gray hats and then back to green and gold whenever she felt like it.

Now the hill that runs down from the shanty of Hatrack the Horse toward the Village of Cream Puffs is a long, long hill. And one morning the old man sat watching and away down at the bottom of the long, long hill he saw four hat boxes. Somebody was coming to call on him. And he knew it was Dippy the Wisp.

The hat boxes came up the hill. He saw them stop once, stop twice, stop more times. So he knew Dippy the Wisp was changing hats, changing from green and gold to purple and gray and then back to green and gold.

When at last she got to the top of the hill and came to the shanty of Hatrack the Horse, she said to him, "Make up a story and tell me. Make up the story about umbrellas. You have traveled all over the Rootabaga Country, you have seen so many umbrellas, and such won-

56

derful umbrellas. Make me up a big elegant story about umbrellas."

So Hatrack the Horse took his hat *off* his head, reached around and hung it *on* one of the shoulder bones sticking out behind on his back. And the old man looked with a far-away look down the long, long hill running from his shanty toward the Village of Cream Puffs. Then he told her this story:

One summer afternoon I came home and found all the umbrellas sitting in the kitchen, with straw hats on, telling each other who they are.

The umbrella that feeds the fishes fresh buns every morning stood up and said, "I am the umbrella that feeds the fishes fresh buns every morning."

The umbrella that fixes the clocks free of charge stood up and said, "I am the umbrella that fixes the clocks free of charge."

The umbrella that peels the potatoes with a

pencil and makes a pink ink with the peelings, stood up and said, "I am the umbrella that peels the potatoes with a pencil and makes a pink ink with the peelings."

The umbrella that eats the rats with pepper and salt and a clean napkin every morning, stood up and said, "I am the umbrella that eats the rats with pepper and salt and a clean napkin every morning."

The umbrella that washes the dishes with a wiper and wipes the dishes with a washer every morning stood up and said, "I am the umbrella that washes the dishes with a wiper and wipes the dishes with a washer every morning."

The umbrella that covers the chimney with a dishpan before it rains stood up and said, "I am the umbrella that covers the chimney with a dishpan before it rains."

The umbrella that runs to the corner to get corners for the handkerchiefs stood up and said, "I am the umbrella that runs to the corner to get corners for the handkerchiefs."

Now while the umbrellas are all sitting in the kitchen with their straw hats on telling each other who they are, there comes a big black stranger of an umbrella, walking into the kitchen without opening the door, walking in without knocking, without asking anybody, without telling anybody beforehand.

"Since we are telling each other who we are," said the stranger, "since we are telling each other who we are, I am going to tell you who I am.

"I am the umbrella that holds up the sky. I am the umbrella the rain comes through. I am the umbrella that tells the sky when to begin raining and when to stop raining.

"I am the umbrella that goes to pieces when the wind blows and then puts itself together again when the wind goes down. I am the first umbrella, the last umbrella, the one and

59

only umbrella all other umbrellas are named after, first, last and always."

When the stranger finished this speech telling who he was and where he came from, all the other umbrellas sat still for a little while, to be respectful.

Then they all got up, took off their straw hats, walked up to the stranger and laid those straw hats at his feet. They wanted to show him they had respect for him. Then they all walked out, first the umbrella that feeds the fishes fresh buns every morning, then the umbrella that fixes the clocks free of charge, then the umbrella that peels the potatoes with a pencil and makes pink ink with the peelings, then the umbrella that eats the rats with pepper and salt and a clean napkin, then the umbrella that washes the dishes with a wiper and wipes the dishes with a washer, then the umbrella that covers the chimney with a dishpan before it rains, then the umbrella that

runs to the corner to get corners for the handkerchiefs. They all laid their straw hats at
the feet of the stranger because he came without knocking or telling anybody beforehand
and because he said he is the umbrella that
holds up the sky, that big umbrella the rain
goes through first of all, the first and the last
umbrella.

That was the way Hatrack the Horse finished his story for Dippy the Wisp. She was
changing hats, getting ready to go.

The old man put his loose bony arms around
her and kissed her for a good-by. And she
put her little dimpled arms around his neck
and kissed him for a good-by.

And the last he saw of her that day she was
walking far away down at the bottom of the
long, long hill that stretches from Hatrack's
shanty toward the Village of Cream Puffs.

And twice going down the long hill she

How Six Umbrellas Took Off Hats

stopped and changed hats, opening and shut-
ting the hat boxes, and changing hats from
green and gold to purple and gray and back
to green and gold.

How Bozo the Button Buster Busted All His Buttons When a Mouse Came

One summer evening the stars in the summer sky seemed to be moving with fishes, cats and rabbits.

It was that summer evening three girls came to the shanty of Hatrack the Horse. He asked each one, "What is your name?" And they answered, first, "Me? My name is Deep Red Roses"; second, "Me? My name is The Beans are Burning"; and last of all, "Me? My name is Sweeter Than the Bees Humming."

How Bozo the Button Buster Busted

And the old man fastened a yellow rose for luck in the hair of each one and said, "You ought to be home now."

"After you tell us a story," they reminded him.

"I can only tell you a sad story all mixed up to-night," he reminded them, "because all day to-day I have been thinking about Bozo the Button Buster."

"Tell us about Bozo the Button Buster," said the girls, feeling in their hair and fixing the yellow roses.

The old man sat down on the front steps. His eyes swept away off toward a corner of the sky heavy with mist where it seemed to be moving with firetails, fishes, cats, and rabbits of slow changing stars.

"Bozo had buttons all over him," said the old man, "the buttons on Bozo fitted so tight, and there were so many buttons, that sometimes when he took his lungs full of new wind to go

64

on talking a button would bust loose and fly into the face of whoever he was speaking to. Sometimes when he took new wind into his lungs two buttons would bust loose and fly into the faces of two people he was speaking to.

"So people said, 'Isn't it queer how buttons fly loose when Bozo fills his lungs with wind to go on speaking?' After a while everybody called him Bozo the Button Buster.

"Now, you must understand, Bozo was different from other people. He had a string tied to him. It was a long string hanging down with a knot in the end. He used to say, 'Sometimes I forget where I am; then I feel for the string tied to me, and I follow the string to where it is tied to me; then I know where I am again.'

"Sometimes when Bozo was speaking and a button busted loose, he would ask, 'Was that a mouse? Was that a mouse?' And sometimes he said to people, 'I'll talk with you— *if you haven't got a mouse in your pocket.*'

How Bozo the Button Buster Busted

"The last day Bozo ever came to the Village of Cream Puffs, he stood on the public square and he was all covered with buttons, more buttons than ever before, and all the buttons fitting tight, and five, six buttons busting loose and flying into the air whenever he took his lungs full of wind to go on speaking.

" 'When the sky began to fall who was it ran out and held up the sky?' he sang out. 'It was me, it was me ran out and held up the sky when the sky began to fall.'

" 'When the blue came off the sky, where did they get the blue to put on the sky to make it blue again? It was me, it was me picked the bluebirds and the blue pigeons to get the blue to fix the sky.'

" 'When it rains now it rains umbrellas first so everybody has an umbrella for the rain afterward. Who fixed that? I did—Bozo the Button Buster.'

" 'Who took the rainbow off the sky and put it back again in a hurry? That was me.'

66

The mouse bit the knot and cut it loose

" 'Who turned all the barns upside down and then put them right side up again? I did that.'

" 'Who took the salt out of the sea and put it back again? Who took the fishes out of the sea and put them back again? That was me.'

" 'Who started the catfish fighting the cats? Who made the slippery elms slippery? Who made the King of the Broken Bottles a wanderer wandering over the world mumbling, "Easy, easy"? Who opened the windows of the stars and threw fishes, cats and rabbits all over the frames of the sky? I did, I did, I did.'

"All the time Bozo kept on speaking the buttons kept on busting because he had to stop so often to fill his lungs with new wind to go on speaking. The public square was filled with piles of buttons that kept busting off from Bozo the Button Buster that day.

"And at last a mouse came, a sneaking, slippery, quick little mouse. He ran with a flash to the string tied to Bozo, the long string hanging down with a knot in the end. He bit the knot and cut it loose. He slit the string with his teeth as Bozo cried, 'Ai! Ai! Ai!'

"The last of all the buttons busted loose off Bozo. The clothes fell off. The people came up to see what was happening to Bozo. There was nothing in the clothes. The man inside the clothes was gone. All that was left was buttons and a few clothes.

"Since then whenever it rains umbrellas first so everybody has an umbrella for the rain afterward, or if the sky looks like it is falling, or if a barn turns upside down, or if the King of the Broken Bottles comes along mumbling, 'Easy, easy,' or if firetails, fishes, cats and rabbits come on the sky in the night, or if a button busts loose and flies into somebody's face, people remember Bozo the Button Buster."

When the three girls started home, each one

70

All His Buttons When a Mouse Came

said to Hatrack the Horse, "It looks dark and lonesome on the prairie, but you put a yellow rose in my hair for luck—and I won't be scared after I get home."

4. Two Stories About Four Boys Who Had Different Dreams.

People: Googler
Gaggler
Twins
The Family Doctor
The Father of the Twins
The Mother of the Twins
Pen Wipers and Pencil Sharp-
eners
Smokestacks and Monkey
Wrenches
Monkey Faces on the Monkey
Wrenches
Left-Handed Monkey
Wrenches

Potato Face Blind Man
Ax Me No Questions
Johnny the Wham
Joe the Wimp
Grasshoppers
Thousand Dollar Bills
Brass Doors
Lizzie Lazarus

How Googler and Gaggler, the Two Christmas Babies, Came Home with Monkey Wrenches

1

Two babies came one night in snowstorm weather, came to a tar paper shack on a cinder patch next the railroad yards on the edge of the Village of Liver-and-Onions.

The family doctor came that night, came with a bird of a spizz car throwing a big spotlight of a headlight through the snow of the snowstorm on the prairie.

"Twins," said the doctor. "Twins," said

the father and mother. And the wind as it shook the tar paper shack and shook the doors and the padlocks on the doors of the tar paper shack, the wind seemed to be howling softly, "Twins, twins."

Six days and Christmas Eve came. The mother of the twins lit two candles, two little two-for-a-nickel candles in each little window. And the mother handed the father the twins and said, "Here are your Christmas presents." The father took the two baby boys and laughed, "Twice times twice is twice."

The two little two-for-a-nickel candles sputtered in each little window that Christmas Eve, and at last sputtered and went out, leaving the prairies dark and lonesome. The father and the mother of the twins sat by the window, each one holding a baby.

Every once in a while they changed babies so as to hold a different twin. And every time they changed they laughed at each other, "Twice times twice is twice."

76

Came Home with Monkey Wrenches

One baby was called Googler, the other Gaggler. The two boys grew up, and hair came on their bald red heads. Their ears, wet behind, got dry. They learned how to pull on their stockings and shoes and tie their shoe-strings. They learned at last how to take a handkerchief and hold it open and blow their noses.

Their father looked at them growing up and said, "I think you'll make a couple of peanut-wagon men pouring hot butter into popcorn sacks."

The family doctor saw the rashes and the itches and the measles and the whooping cough come along one year and another. He saw the husky Googler and the husky Gaggler throw off the rashes and the itches and the measles and the whooping cough. And the family doctor said, "They will go far and see much, and they will never be any good for sitting with the sitters and knitting with the knitters."

Googler and Gaggler grew up and turned

handsprings going to school in short pants, whistling with school books under their arms. They went barefooted and got stickers in their hair and teased cats and killed snakes and climbed apple trees and threw clubs up walnut trees and chewed slippery ellum. They stubbed their toes and cut their feet on broken bottles and went swimming in brickyard ponds and came home with their backs sunburnt so the skin peeled off. And before they went to bed every night they stood on their heads and turned flip-flops.

One morning early in spring the young frogs were shooting silver spears of little new songs up into the sky. Strips of fresh young grass were beginning to flick the hills and spot the prairie with flicks and spots of new green. On that morning, Googler and Gaggler went to school with fun and danger and dreams in their eyes.

They came home that day and told their mother, "There is a war between the pen wipers and the pencil sharpeners. Millions of pen wipers and millions of pencil sharpeners are marching against each other, marching and singing, *Hayfoot, strawfoot, bellyful o' bean soup.* The pen wipers and the pencil sharpeners, millions and millions, are marching with drums, drumming, *Ta rum, ta rum, ta rum tum tum.* The pen wipers say, No matter how many million ink spots it costs and no matter how many million pencil sharpeners we kill, we are going to kill and kill till the last of the pencil sharpeners is killed. The pencil sharpeners say, No matter how many million shavings it costs, no matter how many million pen wipers we kill, we are going to kill and kill till the last of the pen wipers is killed."

The mother of Googler and Gaggler listened, her hands folded, her thumbs under her chin, her eyes watching the fun and the danger and the dreams in the eyes of the two boys. And she said, "Me, oh, my—but those pen

wipers and pencil sharpeners hate each other."
And she turned her eyes toward the flicks and
spots of new green grass coming on the hills
and the prairie, and she let her ears listen to
the young frogs shooting silver spears of little
songs up into the sky that day.

And she told her two boys, "Pick up your
feet now and run. Go to the grass, go to the
new green grass. Go to the young frogs and
ask them why they are shooting songs up into
the sky this early spring day. Pick up your
feet now and run."

2

At last Googler and Gaggler were big boys,
big enough to pick the stickers out of each
other's hair, big enough to pick up their feet
and run away from anybody who chased them.

One night they turned flip-flops and handsprings and climbed up on top of a peanut
wagon where a man was pouring hot butter

They went to sleep on top of the wagon

into popcorn sacks. They went to sleep on top of the wagon. Googler dreamed of teasing cats, killing snakes, climbing apple trees and stealing apples. Gaggler dreamed of swimming in brickyard ponds and coming home with his back sunburnt so the skin peeled off.

They woke up with heavy gunnysacks in their arms. They climbed off the wagon and started home to their father and mother lugging the heavy gunnysacks on their backs. And they told their father and mother:

"We ran away to the Thimble Country where the people wear thimble hats, where the women wash dishes in thimble dishpans, where the men go to work with thimble shovels.

"We saw a war, the left-handed people against the right-handed. And the smoke-stacks did all the fighting. They all had monkey wrenches and they tried to wrench each other to pieces. And they had monkey

83

faces on the monkey wrenches—to scare each other.

"All the time they were fighting the Thimble people sat looking on, the thimble women with thimble dishpans, the thimble men with thimble shovels. They waved handkerchiefs to each other, some left-hand handkerchiefs, and some right-hand handkerchiefs. They sat looking till the smokestacks with their monkey wrenches wrenched each other all to pieces."

Then Googler and Gaggler opened the heavy gunnysacks. "Here," they said, "here is a left-handed monkey wrench, here is a right-handed monkey wrench. And here is a monkey wrench with a monkey face on the handle—to scare with."

Now the father and mother of Googler and Gaggler wonder how they will end up. The family doctor keeps on saying, "They will go far and see much but they will never sit with the sitters and knit with the knitters." And sometimes when their father looks at them, he says what he said the Christmas Eve when the two-for-a-nickel candles stood two by two in the windows, "Twice times twice is twice."

How Johnny the Wham Sleeps in Money All the Time and Joe the Wimp Shines and Sees Things

Once the Potato Face Blind Man began talking about arithmetic and geography, where numbers come from and why we add and subtract before we multiply, when the first fractions and decimal points were invented, who gave the rivers their names, and why some rivers have short names slipping off the tongue easy as whistling, and why other rivers have long names wearing the stub ends off lead pencils.

How Johnny the Wham

The girl, Ax Me No Questions, asked the old man if boys always stay in the home towns where they are born and grow up, or whether boys pack their packsacks and go away somewhere else after they grow up. This question started the old man telling about Johnny the Wham and Joe the Wimp and things he remembered about them:

Johnny the Wham and Joe the Wimp are two boys who used to live here in the Village of Liver-and-Onions before they went away. They grew up here, carving their initials, J. W., on wishbones and peanuts and wheelbarrows. And if anybody found a wishbone or a peanut or a wheelbarrow with the initials, J. W., carved on it, he didn't know whether it was Johnny the Wham or Joe the Wimp.

They met on summer days, put their hands in their pockets and traded each other grasshoppers learning to say yes and no. One kick and a spit meant yes. Two kicks and a spit

meant no. One two three, four five six of a
kick and a spit meant the grasshopper was
counting and learning numbers.

They promised what they were going to
do after they went away from the village.
Johnny the Wham said, "I am going to sleep
in money up to my knees with thousand dollar
bills all over me for a blanket." Joe the
Wimp said, "I am going to see things and
shine, and I am going to shine and see
things."

They went away. They did what they
said. They went up into the grasshopper
country near the Village of Eggs Over where
the grasshoppers were eating the corn in the
fields without counting how much. They
stayed in those fields till those grasshoppers
learned to say yes and no and learned to count.
One kick and a spit meant yes. Two kicks and
a spit meant no. One two three, four five six
meant the grasshoppers were counting and
learning numbers. The grasshoppers, after

that, eating ears of corn in the fields, were counting how many and how much.

To-day Johnny the Wham sleeps in a room full of money in the big bank in the Village of Eggs Over. The room where he sleeps is the room where they keep the thousand dollar bills. He walks in thousand dollar bills up to his knees at night before he goes to bed on the floor. A bundle of thousand dollar bills is his pillow. He covers himself like a man in a haystack or a strawstack, with thousand dollar bills. The paper money is piled around him in armfuls and sticks up and stands out around him the same as hay or straw.

And Lizzie Lazarus, who talked with him in the Village of Eggs Over last week, she says Johnny the Wham told her, "There is music in thousand dollar bills. Before I go to sleep at night and when I wake up in the morning, I listen to their music. They whisper and cry, they sing little oh-me, oh-my songs as they wriggle and rustle next to each other. A few with dirty faces, with torn ears, with patches and finger and thumb prints on their faces, they cry and whisper so it hurts to hear them. And often they shake all over, laughing.

"I heard one dirty thousand dollar bill say to another spotted with patches and thumb prints, 'They kiss us welcome when we come, they kiss us sweet good-by when we go.'

"They cry and whisper and laugh about things and special things and extra extra special things—pigeons, ponies, pigs, special pigeons, ponies, pigs, extra extra special pigeons, ponies, pigs—cats, pups, monkeys, big bags of cats, pups, monkeys, extra extra big bags of special cats, pups, monkeys—jewelry, ice cream, bananas, pie, hats, shoes, shirts, dust pans, rat traps, coffee cups, handkerchiefs, safety pins—diamonds, bottles and big front doors with bells on—they cry and whisper and laugh about these things—and it never hurts unless the dirty thousand dollar bills with torn ears and patches on their faces say to each other,

'They kiss us welcome when we come, they kiss us sweet good-by when we go.' "

The old Potato Face sat saying nothing. He fooled a little with the accordion keys as if trying to make up a tune for the words, "They kiss us welcome when we come, they kiss us sweet good-by when we go."

Ax Me No Questions looked at him with a soft look and said softly, "Now maybe you'll tell about Joe the Wimp." And he told her:

Joe the Wimp shines the doors in front of the bank. The doors are brass, and Joe the Wimp stands with rags and ashes and chamois skin keeping the brass shining.

"The brass shines slick and shows everything on the street like a looking glass," he told Lizzie Lazarus last week. "If pigeons, ponies, pigs, come past, or cats, pups, monkeys, or jewelry, ice cream, bananas, pie, hats, shoes, shirts, dust pans, rat traps, coffee cups, handkerchiefs, safety pins, or diamonds, bottles, and big front doors with bells on, Joe the Wimp sees them in the brass.

"I rub on the brass doors, and things begin to jump into my hands out of the shine of the brass. Faces, chimneys, elephants, yellow humming birds, and blue cornflowers, where I have seen grasshoppers sleeping two by two and two by two, they all come to the shine of the brass on the doors when I ask them to. If you shine brass hard, and wish as hard as the brass wishes, and keep on shining and wishing, then always things come jumping into your hands out of the shine of the brass."

"So you see," said the Potato Face Blind Man to Ax Me No Questions, "sometimes the promises boys make when they go away come true afterward."

"They got what they asked for—now will they keep it or leave it?" said Ax Me.

"Only the grasshoppers can answer that,"

93

was the old man's reply. "The grasshoppers are older. They know more about jumps. And especially grasshoppers that say yes and no and count one two three, four five six."

And he sat saying nothing, fooling with the accordion keys as if trying to make up a tune for the words, "They kiss us welcome when we come, they kiss us sweet good-by when we go."

5. Two Stories Told by the Potato Face Blind Man About Two Girls with Red Hearts.

People: Blixie Bimber
The Potato Face Blind Man
Shoulder Straps
High High Over
Six Bits
Deep Red Roses
A Clock
A Looking Glass
Baggage

Pink Peony
Spuds the Ballplayer
Four Moon
Peacocks
Frogs
Oranges
Yellow Silk Handkerchiefs

How Deep Red Roses Goes Back and Forth Between the Clock and the Looking Glass

One morning when big white clouds were shouldering each other's shoulders, rolling on the rollers of a big blue sky, Blixie Bimber came along where the Potato Face Blind Man sat shining the brass bickerjiggers on his accordion.

"Do you like to shine up the brass bicker-jiggers?" asked Blixie.

"Yes," he answered. "One time a long time ago the brass bickerjiggers were gold, but they stole the gold away when I wasn't looking."

He blinked the eyelids over his eyeballs and said, "I thank them because they took gold they wanted. Brass feels good to my fingers the same as gold." And he went on shining up the brass bickerjiggers on the accordion, humming a little line of an old song, "To-morrow will never catch up with yesterday because yesterday started sooner."

"Seems like a nice morning with the sun spilling bushels of sunshine," he said to Blixie, who answered, "Big white clouds are shouldering each other's shoulders rolling on the rollers of a big blue sky."

"Seems like it's April all over again," he murmured, almost like he wasn't talking at all.

"Seems just that way—April all over again," murmured Blixie, almost like she wasn't talking at all.

Forth Between Clock and Looking Glass

So they began drifting, the old man drifting his way, the girl drifting her way, till he drifted into a story. And the story he told was like this and in these words:

"Deep Red Roses was a lovely girl with blue skylights like the blue skylights of early April in her eyes. And her lips reminded people of deep red roses waiting in the cool of the summer evening.

"She met Shoulder Straps one day when she was young yet. He promised her. And she promised him. But he went away. One of the long wars between two short wars took him. In a far away country, then, he married another girl. And he didn't come back to Deep Red Roses.

"Next came High High Over, one day when she was young yet. A dancer he was, going from one city to another city to dance, spending his afternoons and evenings and late nights dancing, and sleeping in the morning till noon. And when he promised she promised. But he went away to another city and after that another city. And he married one woman and then another woman. Every year there came a new story about one of the new wives of High High Over, the dancer. And while she was young yet, Deep Red Roses forgot all about her promise and the promise of High High Over, the dancer who ran away from her.

"Six Bits was the next to come along. And he was not a soldier nor a dancer nor anything special. He was a careless man, changing from one job to another, changing from paper-hanging to plastering, from fixing shingle roofs where the shingles were ripped to opening cans with can openers.

"Six Bits gave Deep Red Roses his promise and she gave him her promise. But he was always late keeping his promise. When the wedding was to be Tuesday he didn't come till Wednesday. If it was Friday he came Saturday. And there wasn't any wedding.

"So Deep Red Roses said to herself, 'I am going away and learn, I am going away and talk with the wives of High High Over, the dancer, and maybe if I go far enough I will find the wife of Shoulder Straps, the soldier— and maybe the wives of the men who promised me will tell me how to keep promises kept.'

"She packed her baggage till her baggage was packed so full there was room for only one more thing. So she had to decide whether to put a *clock* or whether to put a *looking glass* in her baggage.

" 'My head tells me to carry the clock so I can always tell if I am early or late,' she said to herself. 'But my heart tells me to carry a looking glass so I can look at my face and tell if I am getting older or younger.'

"At last she decides to take the clock and

leave the looking glass—because her head says so. She starts away. She goes through the door, she is out of the house, she goes to the street, she starts up the street.

"Then her heart tells her to go back and change the clock for the looking glass. She goes back up the street, through the door, into the house, into her room. Now she stands in front of the clock and the looking glass saying, 'To-night I sleep home here one more night, and to-morrow morning I decide again.'

"And now every morning Deep Red Roses decides with her head to take the clock. She takes the clock and starts away and then comes back because her heart decides she must have the looking glass.

"If you go to her house this morning you will see her standing in the doorway with blue skylights like the blue sky of early April in her eyes, and lips that remind you of deep red roses in the cool of the evening in summer.

102

Forth Between Clock and Looking Glass

You will see her leave the doorway and go out of the gate with the clock in her hands. Then if you wait you will see her come back through the gate, into the door, back to her room where she puts down the clock and takes up the looking glass.

"After that she decides to wait until to-morrow morning to decide again what to decide. Her head tells her one thing, her heart tells her another. Between the two she stays home. Sometimes she looks at her face in the looking glass and says to herself, 'I am young yet and while I am young I am going to do my own deciding.' "

Blixie Bimber fingered the end of her chin with her little finger and said, "It is a strange story. It has a stab in it. It would hurt me if I couldn't look up at the big white clouds shouldering their shoulders, rolling on the rollers of the big blue sky."

103

Deep Red Roses Goes Back and Forth

"It is a good story to tell when April is here all over again—and I am shining up the brass bickerjiggers on my accordion," said the Potato Face Blind Man.

How Pink Peony Sent Spuds, the Ball-player, Up to Pick Four Moons

Early one summer evening the moon was hanging in the tree-tops. There was a lisp of leaves. And the soft shine of the moon sifting down seemed to have something to say to the lisp of the leaves.

The girl named Blixie Bimber came that particular summer evening to the corner where the Potato Face Blind Man sat with his accordion. She came walking slow and thoughtful to where he was sitting in the

105

evening shadows. And she told him about the summer moon in the tree-tops, the lisp of the leaves, and the shine of the moon trying to tell something to the lisp of the leaves.

The old man leaned back, fumbled the keys of his accordion, and said it loosened up things he remembered far back.

"On an evening like this, every tree has a moon all of its own for itself—if you climb up in a thousand trees this evening you can pick a thousand moons," the old man murmured. "You remind me to-night about secrets swimming deep in me."

And after hesitating a little—and thinking a little—and then hesitating some more—the old man started and told this story:

There was a girl I used to know, one time, named Pink Peony. She was a girl with cheeks and lips the peonies talked about.

When she passed a bush of peonies, some of

the flowers would whisper, "She is lovelier than we are." And the other peonies would answer in a whisper, "It *must* be so, it . . must . . be . . *so.*"

Now there was a ballplayer named Spuds, came one night to take her riding, out to a valley where the peacocks always cry before it rains, where the frogs always gamble with the golden dice after midnight.

And out in that valley they came to a tall tree shooting spraggly to the sky. And high up in the spraggly shoots, where the lisp of the leaves whispers, there a moon had drifted down and was caught in the branches.

"Spuds, climb up and pick *that* moon for me," Pink Peony sang reckless. And the ballplayer jumped out of the car, climbed up the tall tree, up and up till he was high and far in the spraggly branches where the moon had drifted down and was caught.

Climbing down, he handed the girl a silver

hat full of peach-color pearls. She laid it on the back seat of the car where it would be safe. And they drove on.

They came to another tall tree shooting spraggly to the sky. And high up the moon was caught.

"Pick *that* one, Spuds," Peony sang reckless again. And when he came climbing down he handed her a circle of gold with a blood-color autumn leaf. And they put it on the back seat of the car where it would be safe. Then they drove on.

"Spuds, you are good to me," said Pink Peony, when he climbed another tree shooting spraggly high in the sky, and came down with a brass pansy sprinkled with two rainbows, for her. She put it on the back seat where it would be safe. And they drove on.

One time more Spuds climbed up and came down with what he picked, up where the moon was caught in the high spraggly branches. "An Egyptian collar frozen in diamond cobwebs, for you," he said. "You are a dear, Spuds," she said, reckless, with a look into his eyes. She laid the Egyptian collar frozen in diamond cobwebs on the back seat of the car where it would be safe—and they drove on.

They listened a while, they stopped the car and listened a longer while, to the frogs gambling with golden dice after midnight.

And when at last they heard the peacocks crying, they knew it was going to rain. So they drove home.

And while the peacocks were crying, and just before they started home, they looked in the back seat of the car at the silver hat full of peach-color pearls, the circle of gold with a blood-color autumn leaf, the brass pansy sprinkled with two rainbows, the Egyptian collar frozen in diamond cobwebs.

Driving home, the spray of a violet dawn was on the east sky. And it was nearly daylight when they drove up to the front door of

109

Pink Peony's home. She ran into the house
to get a basket to carry the presents in. She
came running out of the house with a basket
to carry the presents in.

She looked in the back seat; she felt with
her hands and fingers all over the back seat.

In the back seat she could find only four
oranges. They opened the oranges and in each
orange they found a yellow silk handkerchief.

To-day, if you go to the house where Pink
Peony and Spuds are living, you will find four
children playing there, each with a yellow
silk handkerchief tied around the neck in a
mystic slip knot.

Each child has a moon face and a moon
name. And sometimes their father and mother
pile them all into a car and they ride out to
the valley where the peacocks always cry
before it rains—and where the frogs always
gamble with golden dice after midnight.

And what they look longest at is a summer
moon hanging in the tree-tops, when there is

a lisp of leaves, and the shine of the moon and the lisp of the leaves seem to be telling each other something.

So the Potato Face came to a finish with his story. Blixie Bimber kissed him good-night on the nose, saying, "You loosened up beautiful to-night."

6. Three Stories About Moonlight, Pigeons, Bees, Egypt, Jesse James, Spanish Onions, the Queen of the Cracked Heads, the King of the Paper Sacks.

People: Dippy the Wisp
Slip Me Liz
The Potato Face Blind Man
Egypt
Jesse James
Spanish Onions
The Queen of the Cracked Heads
The King of the Paper Sacks
The Queen of the Empty Hats
Hot Balloons
A Snoox
A Gringo
Sweetheart Dippies
Nail-eating Rats
Sooners
Boomers

More People:
Cracked Heads
Clock-eating Goats
Baby Alligators
Pink and Purple Peanuts
Empty Hats
Bats, Cats, Rats
Rag Pickers, Rag Handlers
Squirrels, Fish, Baboons, Black Cats
A Steel Car, an Air Car
Gophers

How Dippy the Wisp and Slip Me Liz Came in the Moonshine Where the Potato Face Blind Man Sat with His Accordion

The sky shook a rain down one Saturday night over the people, the postoffice, and the peanut-stand in the Village of Liver-and-Onions.

And after the rain, the sky shook loose a moon so a moonshine came with gold on the rain-pools.

And a west wind came out of the west sky and shook the moonshine gold on the tops of the rainpools.

Dippy the Wisp and Slip Me Liz came, two tough pony girls, two limber prairie girls, in the moonshine humming little humpty dumpty songs.

They came to the postoffice corner where the Potato Face Blind Man sat hugging his accordion, wondering what was next and who and why.

He was saying to himself, "Who was it told me the rats on the moon in the middle of the winter lock their mittens in ice boxes?"

And just then Dippy the Wisp and Slip Me Liz came flipping along saying, "It is a misty moisty evening in the moonshine, isn't it?"

And he answered, "The moon is a round gold door with silver transoms to-night. Bumble bees and honey bees are chasing each other over the gold door of the moon and up over the silver transoms."

116

Came in the Moonshine

Dippy the Wisp took out a bee-bag, took bees out of the bee-bag, balanced the bees on her thumb, humming a humpty dumpty song. And Slip Me Liz, looking on, joined in on the humpty dumpty song. And, of course, the bees began buzzing and buzzing their *bee* humpty dumpty song.

"Have you fastened names on them?" asked the Potato Face.

"These three on my thumb, these three special blue-violet bees, I put their names on silk white ribbons and tied the ribbons to their knees. This is Egypt—she has inkwells in her ears. This is Jesse James—he puts postage stamps on his nose. This is Spanish Onions— she likes pearl-color handkerchiefs around her yellow neck."

"Bees belong in bee-bags, but these are different," the old man murmured.

"Runaway bees, these are," Dippy the Wisp went on. "They buzz away, they come buzzing back, buzzing home, buzzing secrets, syllables, snitches.

"To-day Egypt came buzzing home with her inkwells in her ears. And Egypt buzzed, 'I flew and flew and I buzzed and buzzed far, far away, till I came where I met the Queen of the Cracked Heads with her head all cracked. And she took me by the foot and took me to the palace of the Cracked Heads with their heads all cracked.

" 'The palace was full of goats walking up and down the stairs, sliding on the banisters eating bingety bing clocks. Before he bites the clock and chews and swallows and eats the bingety bing clock, I noticed, each goat winds up the clock and fixes it to go off bling bling bingety bing, after he eats it down. I noticed that. And the fat, fat, puffy goats, the fat, fat, waddly goats, had extra clocks hung on their horns—and the clocks, tired of waiting, spoke to each other in the bingety bing clock talk. I noticed that too.

She was sitting on a ladder feeding baby clocks to
the baby alligators

Came in the Moonshine

" 'I stayed all morning and I saw them feed the big goats big hunks and the little goats little hunks and the big clocks big bings and the little clocks little bings. At last in the afternoon, the queen of the Cracked Heads came with her cracked head to say good-by to me. She was sitting on a ladder feeding baby clocks to baby alligators, winding the clocks and fixing the bingety bings, so after the baby alligators swallowed the clocks, I heard them singing bling bling bingety bing.

" 'And the Queen was reading the alphabet to the littlest of the baby alligators—and they were saying the alligator A B C while she was saying the A B C of the Cracked Heads. At last she said good-by to me, good-by and come again soon, good-by and stay longer next time.'

" 'When I went out of the door all the baby alligators climbed up the ladder and bingety blinged good-by to me. I buzzed home fast because I was lonesome. I am so, *so* glad to be home again.' "

How Dippy the Wisp and Slip Me Liz

The Potato Face looked up and said, "This is nice as the rats on the moon in the middle of the winter locking their mittens in the ice box. Tell us next about that blue-violet bumblebee, Jesse James."

"Jesse James," said Dippy the Wisp, "Jesse James came buzzing home with a postage stamp on his nose. And Jesse James buzzed, 'I flew and I flew and buzzed and buzzed far, far away till I came where I met the King of the Paper Sacks who lives in a palace of paper sacks. I went inside the palace expecting to see paper sacks everywhere. But instead of paper sacks the palace was full of pink and purple peanuts walking up and down the stairs washing their faces, stitching handkerchiefs.'

" 'In the evening all the pink and purple peanuts put on their overshoes and make paper sacks. The King of the Paper Sacks walks around and around among them saying, "If anybody asks you who I am tell them I am the King of the Paper Sacks." And one little peanut flipped up one time in the King's face and asked, "Say it again—*who* do you think you are?" And it made the King so bitter in his feelings he reached out his hand and with a sweep and a swoop he swept fifty pink and purple peanuts into a paper sack and cried out, "A nickel a sack, a nickel a sack." And he threw them into a trash pile of tin cans.

" 'When I went away he shook hands with me and said, "Good-by, Jesse James, you old buzzer, if anybody asks you tell them you saw the King of the Paper Sacks where he lives.

" 'When I went away from the palace, the doors and the window sills, the corners of the roofs and the eave troughs where the rain runs off, they were all full of pink and purple peanuts standing in their overshoes washing their faces, stitching handkerchiefs, calling good-by to me, good-by and come again, good-by and stay longer next time. Then I came buzzing home because I was lonesome. And I am so, *so* glad to be home again.' "

The Potato Face looked up again and said, "It *is* a misty moisty evening in the moonshine. Now tell us about that blue-violet honeybee, Spanish Onions."

And Dippy the Wisp tied a slipknot in the pearl-color handkerchief around the yellow neck of Spanish Onions and said, "Spanish Onions came buzzing back home with her face dirty and scared and she told us, 'I flew and flew and I buzzed and buzzed till I came where I met the Queen of the Empty Hats. She took me by the foot and took me across the City of the Empty Hats, saying under her breath, "There is a screw loose somewhere, there is a leak in the tank." Fat rats, fat bats, fat cats, came along under empty hats and the Queen always said under her breath, "There is a screw loose somewhere, there is a leak in the tank." In the houses, on the street, riding on the rattlers and the razz cars, the only people were hats, empty hats. When the fat rats changed hats with the fat bats, the hats were empty. When the fat bats changed *those* hats with the fat cats, the hats were empty. I took off my hat and saw it was empty. *I began to feel like an empty hat myself.* I got scared. I jumped loose from the Queen of the Empty Hats and buzzed back home fast. I am so, *so* glad to be home again.' "

The Potato Face sat hugging his accordion. He looked up and said, "Put the bees back in the bee-bag—they buzz too many secrets, syllables and snitches."

"What do you expect when the moon is a gold door with silver transoms?" asked Slip Me Liz.

"Yes," said Dippy the Wisp. "What do you expect when the bumblebees and the honeybees are chasing each other over the gold door of the moon and up over the silver transoms?"

Dippy the Wisp and Slip Me Liz

And the two tough pony girls, the two limber prairie girls, went away humming a little humpty dumpty song across the moonshine gold on the tops of the rainpools.

How Hot Balloons and His Pigeon Daughters Crossed Over into the Rootabaga Country

Hot Balloons was a man who lived all alone among people who sell slips, flips, flicks and chicks by the dozen, by the box, by the box car job lot, back and forth to each other.

Hot Balloons used to open the window in the morning and say to the rag pickers and the rag handlers, "Far, far away the pigeons are calling; far, far away the white wings are dipping in the blue, in the sky blue."

And the rag pickers and the rag handlers looked up from their rag bags and said, "Far, far away the rags are flying; far, far away the rags are whistling in the wind, in the sky wind."

Now two pigeons came walking up to the door, the door knob and the door bell under the window of Hot Balloons. One of the pigeons rang the bell. The other pigeon, too, stepped up to the bell and gave it a ring.

Then they waited, tying the shoe strings on their shoes and the bonnet strings under their chins, while they waited.

Hot Balloons opened the door. And they flew into his hands, one pigeon apiece in each of his hands, flipping and fluttering their wings, calling, "Ka loo, ka loo, ka lo, ka lo," leaving a letter in his hands and then flying away fast.

Hot Balloons stepped out on the front steps to read the letter where the light was good in

One of the pigeons rang the bell

the daylight because it was so early in the morning. The letter was on paper scribbled over in pigeon foot blue handwriting with many secrets and syllables.

After Hot Balloons read the letter, he said to himself, "I wonder if those two pigeons are my two runaway daughters, Dippy the Wisp and Slip Me Liz. When they ran away they said they would cross the Shampoo river and go away into the Rootabaga country to live. And I have heard it is a law of the Rootabaga country whenever a girl crosses the Shampoo river to come back where she used to be, she changes into a pigeon—and she stays a pigeon till she crosses back over the Shampoo river into the Rootabaga country again."

And he shaded his eyes with his hands and looked far, far away in the blue, in the sky blue. And by looking long and hard he saw far, far away in the sky blue, the two white pigeons dipping their wings in the blue, flying fast, circling and circling higher and higher, toward the Shampoo river, toward the Rootabaga country.

"I wonder, I guess, I think so," he said to himself, "I wonder, I think so, it must be those two pigeons are my two runaway daughters, my two girls, Dippy the Wisp and Slip Me Liz."

He took out the letter and read it again right side up, upside down, back and forth. "It is the first time I ever read pigeon foot blue handwriting," he said to himself. And the way he read the letter, it said to him:

Daddy, daddy, daddy, come home to us in the Rootabaga country where the pigeons call ka loo, ka loo, ka lo, ka lo, where the squirrels carry ladders and the wildcats ask riddles and the fish jump out of the rivers and speak to the frying pans, where the baboons take care of the babies and the black cats come and go in orange and gold stockings, where the birds wear rose and purple hats on Monday afternoons up in the skylights in the evening.

(Signed) Dippy the Wisp,
Slip Me Liz.

And reading the letter a second time, Hot Balloons said to himself, "No wonder it is scribbled over the paper in pigeon foot blue handwriting. No wonder it is full of secrets and syllables."

So he jumped into a shirt and a necktie, he jumped into a hat and a vest, and he jumped into a steel car, starting with a snizz and a snoof till it began running smooth and even as a catfoot.

"I will ride to the Shampoo river faster than two pigeons fly," he said. "I will be there."

Which he was. He got there before the two pigeons. But it was no use. For the rain and the rainstorm was working—and the rain and the rainstorm tore down and took and washed away the steel bridge over the Shampoo river.

"Now there is only an air bridge to cross on, and a *steel* car drops down, falls off, falls through, if it runs on an *air* bridge," he said.

Hot Balloons and His Pigeon Daughters

So he was all alone with the rain and the rainstorm all around him—and far as he could see by shading his eyes and looking, there was only the rain and the rainstorm across the river —and the *air* bridge.

While he waited for the rain and the rainstorm to go down, two pigeons came flying into his hands, one apiece into each hand, flipping and fluttering their wings and calling, "Ka loo, ka loo, ka lo, ka lo." And he could tell by the way they began tying the shoestrings on their shoes and the bonnet strings under their chins, they were the same two pigeons ringing the door bell that morning.

They wrote on his thumb-nails in pigeon foot blue handwriting, and he read their handwriting asking him why he didn't cross over the Shampoo river. And he explained, "There is only an *air* bridge to cross on. A *steel* car drops down, falls off, falls through, if it runs on an *air* bridge. Change my *steel* car to an *air* car. Then I can cross the *air* bridge."

Crossed into the Rootabaga Country

The pigeons flipped and fluttered, dipped their wings and called, "Ka loo, ka loo, ka lo, ka lo." And they scribbled their pigeon feet on his thumb-nail—telling him to wait. So the pigeons went flying across the Shampoo river.

They came back with a basket. In the basket was a snoox and a gringo. And the snoox and the gringo took hammers, jacks, flanges, nuts, screws, bearings, ball bearings, axles, axle grease, ax handles, spits, spitters, spitballs and spitfires, and worked.

"It's a hot job," said the snoox to the gringo. "I'll say it's a hot job," said the gringo answering the snoox.

"We'll give this one the merry razoo," said the snoox to the gringo, working overtime and double time. "Yes, we'll put her to the cleaners and shoot her into high," said the gringo, answering the snoox, working overtime and double time.

They changed the steel to air, made an *air*

car out of the *steel* car, put Hot Balloons and the two pigeons into the air car and *drove the air car across the air bridge.*

And nowadays when people talk about it in the Rootabaga country, they say, "The snoox and the gringo drove the air car across the air bridge clean and cool as a whistle in the wind. As soon as the car got off the bridge and over into the Rootabaga country, the two pigeons changed in a flash. And Hot Balloons saw they were his two daughters, his two runaway girls, Dippy the Wisp and Slip Me Liz, standing and smiling at him and looking fresh and free as two fresh fish in a free river, fresh and free as two fresh bimbos in a bamboo tree.

He kissed them both, two long kisses, and while he was kissing them the snoox and the gringo worked double time and overtime and changed the *air* car back into a *steel* car.

And Dippy the Wisp and Slip Me Liz rode in that car—starting with a snizz and a snoof till it began running smooth and even as a catfoot—showing their father, Hot Balloons, where the squirrels carry ladders and the wild-cats ask riddles and the fish jump out of the rivers and speak to the frying pans, where the baboons take care of the babies and the black cats come and go in orange and gold stockings, where the birds wear rose and purple hats on Monday afternoons up in the skylights in the evening.

And often on a Saturday night or a New Year Eve or a Christmas morning, Hot Balloons remembers back how things used to be, and he tells his two girls about the rag pickers and the rag handlers back among the people who sell slips, flips, flicks, and chicks, by the dozen, by the box, by the box car job lot, back and forth to each other.

How Two Sweetheart Dippies Sat in the Moonlight on a Lumber Yard Fence and Heard About the Sooners and the Boomers

Not so very far and not so very near the Village of Liver-and-Onions is a dippy little town where dippy people used to live.

And it was long, long ago the sweetheart dippies stood in their windows and watched the dips of the star dippers in the dip of the sky.

It was the dippies who took the running wild oleander and the cunning wild rambler rose and kept them so the running wild winters let them alone.

"It is easy to be a dippy . . . among the dippies . . . isn't it?" the sweetheart dippies whispered to each other, sitting in the leaf shadows of the oleander, the rambler rose.

The name of this dippy town came by accident. The name of the town is Thumbs Up and it used to be named Thumbs Down and expects to change its name back and forth between Thumbs Up and Thumbs Down.

The running wild oleanders and the running wild rambler roses grow there over the big lumber yards where all the old lumber goes.

The dippies and the dippy sweethearts go out there to those lumber yards and sit on the fence moonlight nights and look at the lumber.

The rusty nails in the lumber get rustier and rustier till they drop out. And whenever they drop out there is always a rat standing under to take the nail in his teeth and chew the nail and eat it.

Heard About Sooners and Boomers

For this is the place the nail-eating rats come to from all over the Rootabaga country. Father rats and mother rats send the young rats there to eat nails and get stronger.

If a young rat comes back from a trip to the lumber yards in Thumbs Up and he meets another young rat going to those lumber yards, they say to each other, "Where have you been?" "To Thumbs Up." "And how do you feel?" *"Hard as nails."*

Now one night two of the dippies, a sweetheart boy and girl, went out to the big lumber yards and sat on the fence and looked at the lumber and the running wild oleanders and the running wild rambler roses.

And they saw two big rusty nails, getting rustier and rustier, drop out of the lumber and drop into the teeth of two young rats.

And the two young rats sat up on their tails there in the moonlight under the oleanders, under the roses, and one of the young rats told the other young rat a story he made up out of his head.

Chewing on the big rusty nail and then swallowing, telling more of the story after swallowing and before beginning to chew the nail again, this is the story he told—and this is the story the two dippies, the two sweethearts sitting on the fence in the moonlight, heard:

Far away where the sky drops down, and the sunsets open doors for the nights to come through—where the running winds meet, change faces and come back—there is a prairie where the green grass grows all around.

And on that prairie the gophers, the black and brown-striped ground squirrels, sit with their backs straight up, sitting on their soft paddy tails, sitting in the spring song murmur of the south wind, saying to each other, "This is the prairie and the prairie belongs to us."

142

Heard About Sooners and Boomers

Now far back in the long time, the gophers came there, chasing each other, playing the-green-grass-grew-all-around, playing cross tag, hop tag, skip tag, billy-be-tag, billy-be-it.

The razorback hogs came then, eating pignuts, potatoes, paw paws, pumpkins. The wild horse, the buffalo, came. The moose, with spraggly branches of antlers spreading out over his head, the moose came—and the fox, the wolf.

The gophers flipped a quick flip-flop back into their gopher holes when the fox, the wolf, came. And the fox, the wolf, stood at the holes and said, "You *look* like rats, you *run* like rats, you *are* rats, rats with stripes. Bah! you are only *rats*. Bah!"

It was the first time anybody said "Bah!" to the gophers. They sat in a circle with their noses up asking, "*What* does this 'Bah!' mean?" And an old timer, with his hair falling off in patches, with the stripes on his soft paddy tail patched with patches, this old

143

timer of a gopher said, " 'Bah!' speaks more than it means whenever it is spoken."

Then the sooners and the boomers came, saying "Bah!" and saying it many new ways, till the fox, the wolf, the moose, the wild horse, the buffalo, the razorback hog picked up their feet and ran away without looking back.

The sooners and boomers began making houses, sod houses, log, lumber, plaster-and-lath houses, stone, brick, steel houses, but most of the houses were lumber with nails to hold the lumber together to keep the rain off and push the wind back and hold the blizzards outside.

In the beginning the sooners and boomers told stories, spoke jokes, made songs, with their arms on each other's shoulders. They dug wells, helping each other get water. They built chimneys together helping each other let the smoke out of their houses. And every year the day before Thanksgiving they went in cahoots with their post hole diggers and dug all the post holes for a year to come. That was in the morning. In the afternoon they took each other's cistern cleaners and cleaned all the cisterns for a year to come. And the next day on Thanksgiving they split turkey wishbones and thanked each other they had all the post holes dug and all the cisterns cleaned for a year to come.

If the boomers had to have broom corn to make brooms the sooners came saying, "Here is your broom corn." If the sooners had to have a gallon of molasses, the boomers came saying, "Here is your gallon of molasses."

They handed each other big duck eggs to fry, big goose eggs to boil, purple pigeon eggs for Easter breakfast. Wagon loads of buff banty eggs went back and forth between the sooners and boomers. And they took big hay-racks full of buff banty hens and traded them for hayracks full of buff banty roosters.

And one time at a picnic, one summer afternoon, the sooners gave the boomers a thousand golden ice tongs with hearts and hands carved on the handles. And the boomers gave the sooners a thousand silver wheelbarrows with hearts and hands carved on the handles.

Then came pigs, pigs, pigs, and more pigs. And the sooners and boomers said the pigs had to be painted. There was a war to decide whether the pigs should be painted pink or green. Pink won.

The next war was to decide whether the pigs should be painted checks or stripes. Checks won. The next war after that was to decide whether the checks should be painted pink or green. Green won.

Then came the longest war of all, up till that time. And this war decided the pigs should be painted both pink and green, both checks and stripes.

They rested then. But it was only a short rest. For then came the war to decide whether peach pickers must pick peaches on Tuesday mornings or on Saturday afternoons. Tuesday mornings won. This was a short war. Then came a long war—to decide whether telegraph pole climbers must eat onions at noon with spoons, or whether dishwashers must keep their money in pig's ears with padlocks pinched on with pincers.

So the wars went on. Between wars they called each other goofs and snoofs, grave robbers, pickpockets, porch climbers, pie thieves, pie face mutts, bums, big bums, big greasy bums, dummies, mummies, rummies, sneezicks, bohunks, wops, snorkies, ditch diggers, peanuts, fatheads, sapheads, pinheads, pickle faces, horse thieves, rubbernecks, big pieces of cheese, big bags of wind, snabs, scabs, and dirty sniveling snitches. Sometimes when they got tired of calling each other names they scratched in the air with their fingers and made faces with their tongues out twisted like pretzels.

After a while, it seemed, there was no corn, no broom corn, no brooms, not even teeny sweepings of corn or broom corn or brooms. And there were no duck eggs to fry, goose eggs to boil, no buff banty eggs, no buff banty hens, no buff banty roosters, no wagons for wagon loads of buff banty eggs, no hayracks for hayrack loads of buff banty hens and buff banty roosters.

And the thousand golden ice tongs the sooners gave the boomers, and the thousand silver wheelbarrows the boomers gave the sooners, both with hearts and hands carved on the handles, they were long ago broken up in one of the early wars deciding pigs must be painted both pink and green with both checks and stripes.

And now, at last, there were no more pigs to paint either pink or green or with checks or stripes. The pigs, pigs, pigs, were gone.

So the sooners and boomers all got lost in the wars or they screwed wooden legs on their stump legs and walked away to bigger, bigger prairies or they started away for the rivers and mountains, stopping always to count how many fleas there were in any bunch of fleas they met. If you see anybody who stops to count the fleas in a bunch of fleas, that is a sign he is either a sooner or a boomer.

So again the gophers, the black and brown striped ground squirrels, sit with their backs straight up, sitting on their soft paddy tails, sitting in the spring song murmur of the south wind, saying, "This is the prairie and the prairie belongs to us."

Far away to-day where the sky drops down and the sunsets open doors for the nights to come through—where the running winds meet, change faces and come back—there the gophers are playing the-green-grass-grew-all-around, playing cross tag, skip tag, hop tag, billy-be-tag, billy-be-it. And sometimes they sit in a circle and ask, "What does this 'Bah!' mean?" And an old timer answers, "'Bah!' speaks more than it means whenever it is spoken."

Two Sweetheart Dippies

That was the story the young rat under the oleanders, under the roses, told the other young rat, while the two sweetheart dippies sat on the fence in the moonlight looking at the lumber and listening.

The young rat who told the story hardly got started eating the nail he was chewing, while the young rat that did the listening chewed up and swallowed down a whole nail.

As the two dippies on the fence looked at the running wild oleander and the running wild rambler roses over the lumber in the moonlight, they said to each other, "It's easy to be a dippy . . . among the dippies . . . isn't it?" And they climbed down from the fence and went home in the moonlight.

7. Two Stories Out of the Tall Grass.

People: John Jack Johannes Humma-
dummaduffer
Feed Box
Eva Evelyn Evangeline Hum-
madummaduffer
Sky Blue
The Harvest Moon
A Haystack Cricket

Baby Moon
Half Moon
Silver Moon

Doorbells, Chimneys, Cellars

The Night Policeman in the
Village of Cream Puffs
Butter Fingers
Three Strikes
Cub Ballplayers

The Haystack Cricket and How Things Are Different Up in the Moon Towns

There is an old man with wrinkles like wrinkled leather on his face living among the cornfields on the rolling prairie near the Shampoo river.

His name is John Jack Johannes Hummadummaduffer. His cronies and the people who know him call him Feed Box.

His daughter is a cornfield girl with hair

shining the way cornsilk shines when the corn is ripe in the fall time. The tassels of cornsilk hang down and blow in the wind with a rusty dark gold, and they seem to get mixed with her hair. Her name is Eva Evelyn Evangeline Hummadummaduffer. And her chums and the people who know her call her Sky Blue.

The eleventh month, November, comes every year to the corn belt on that rolling prairie. The wagons bring the corn from the fields in the harvest days and the cracks in the corncribs shine with the yellow and gold of the corn.

The harvest moon comes, too. They say it stacks sheaves of the November gold moonshine into gold corn shocks on the sky. So they say.

On those mornings in November that time of the year, the old man they call Feed Box sits where the sun shines against the boards of a corncrib.

Are Different Up in the Moon Towns

The girl they call Sky Blue, even though her name is Eva Evelyn Evangeline Hummadummaduffer, she comes along one November morning. Her father is sitting in the sun with his back against a corncrib. And he tells her he always sits there every year listening to the mice in the cornfields getting ready to move into the big farmhouse.

"When the frost comes and the corn is husked and put in the corncribs, the fields are cleaned and the cold nights come. Papa mouse and mama mouse tell the little ones it is time to sneak into the cellar and the garret and the attic of the farmhouse," said Feed Box to Sky Blue.

"I am listening," she said, "and I can hear the papa mouse and the mama mouse telling the little ones how they will find rags and paper and wool and splinters and shavings and hair, and they will make warm nests for the winter in the big farmhouse—if no kits, cats nor kittycats get them."

The Haystack Cricket and How Things

The old man, Feed Box, rubbed his back and his shoulders against the boards of the corncrib and washed his hands almost as if he might be washing them in the gold of the autumn sunshine. Then he told this happening:

This time of the year, when the mouse in the fields whispers so I can hear him, I remember one November when I was a boy.

One night in November when the harvest moon was shining and stacking gold cornshocks in the sky, I got lost. Instead of going home I was going away from home. And the next day and the next night instead of going home I was going away from home.

That second night I came to a haystack where a yellow and gold cricket was singing. And he was singing the same songs the crickets sing in the haystacks back home where the Hummadummaduffers raise hay and corn, in the corn belt near the Shampoo river.

And he told me, this cricket did, he told me when he listened soft if everything was still in the grass and the sky, he could hear golden crickets singing in the cornshocks the harvest moon had stacked in the sky.

I went to sleep listening to the singing of the yellow and gold crickets in that haystack. It was early in the morning, long before daylight, I guess, the two of us went on a trip away from the haystack.

We took a trip. The yellow and gold cricket led the way. "It is the call of the harvest moon," he said to me in a singing whisper. "We are going up to the moon towns where the harvest moon stacks the cornshocks on the sky."

We came to a little valley in the sky. And the harvest moon had slipped three little towns into that valley, three little towns named Half Moon, Baby Moon, and Silver Moon.

In the town of Half Moon they *look* out of the doors and *come in* at the windows. So they have taken all the doorbells off the doors and put them on the windows. Whenever we rang a doorbell we went to a window.

In the town of Baby Moon they had windows on the chimneys so the smoke can look out of the window and see the weather before it comes out over the top of the chimney. And whenever the chimneys get tired of being stuck up on the top of the roof, the chimneys climb down and dance in the cellar. We saw five chimneys climb down and join hands and bump heads and dance a laughing chimney dance.

In the town of Silver Moon the cellars are not satisfied. They say to each other, "We are tired of being under, always under." So the cellars slip out from being under, always under. They slip out and climb up on top of the roof.

And that was all we saw up among the moon towns of Half Moon, Baby Moon and Silver Moon. We had to get back to the haystack so as to get up in the morning after our night sleep.

"This time of the year I always remember that November," said the old man, Feed Box, to his daughter, Sky Blue.

And Sky Blue said, "I am going to sleep in a haystack sometime in November just to see if a yellow and gold cricket will come with a singing whisper and take me on a trip to where the doorbells are on the windows and the chimneys climb down and dance."

The old man murmured, "Don't forget the cellars tired of being under, always under."

Why the Big Ball Game Between Hot Grounders and the Grand Standers Was a Hot Game

Up near the Village of Cream Puffs is a string of ball towns hiding in the tall grass. Passengers in the railroad trains look out of the windows and the tall grass stands up so they can't see the ball towns. But the ball towns are there and the tall grass is full of pitchers, catchers, basemen, fielders, short stops, sluggers, southpaws and backstops. They play ball till dark and after dark they talk ball. The big fast ballplayers in the Rootabaga Country all come from these ball towns in the tall grass.

The towns used to have names like names in books. But now the names are all like ball talk: Knock the Cover Off, Home Plate, Chest Protector, Grand Stand, Nine Innings, Three Balls and Two Strikes, Bases Full and Two Out, Big League, Bush League, Hot Grounder, Out Drop, Bee Liner, Muffs and Pick Ups, Slide Kelly Slide, Paste It On the Nose.

Now the Night Policeman in the Village of Cream Puffs stopped in at the Cigar Store one night and a gang of cub ballplayers loafing and talking ball talk asked him if there was anything in the wind. And he told them this happening:

"I was sitting on the front steps of the postoffice last night thinking how many letters get lost and how many letters never get answered. A ballplayer came along with a package and said his name was Butter Fingers and he was the heavy hitter, the hard slugger, for the Grand Stand ball team playing a championship game the day before with the Hot Grounders ball team. He came to the Village of Cream Puffs the day before the game, found a snoox and a gringo and got the snoox and the gringo to make him *a home run shirt.* Wearing a home run shirt, he told me, you knock a home run every time you come to bat. He said he knocked a home run every time he came to bat, and it was his home runs won the game for the Grand Standers. He was carrying a package and said the home run shirt was in the package and he was taking it back to the snoox and the gringo because he promised he wouldn't keep it, and it belonged to the snoox and the gringo and they only rented it to him for the championship game. The last I saw of him he was hot-footing it pitty-pat pitty-pat up the street with the package.

"Well, I just said tra-la-loo to Butter Fingers when along comes another ballplayer. He had a package too, and he said his name was Three Strikes, and he was the left-handed southpaw pitcher for the Hot Grounders team the day before playing a game against the Grand Stand team. He said he knew unless he put over some classy pitching the game was lost and everything was goose eggs. So he came to the Village of Cream Puffs the day before the game, found a snoox and a gringo and got the snoox and the gringo to make him *a spitball shirt*. A spitball looks easy, he told me, but it has smoke and whiskers and nobody can touch it. He said he handed the Grand Standers a line of inshoots close to their chins and they never got to first base. Three Strikes was carrying a package and he said the spitball shirt was in the package, and he was taking it back to the snoox and the gringo because he promised he wouldn't keep it and it belonged to the snoox and the gringo and they only rented it to him. The last I saw of him he was hot-footing it pitty-pat pitty-pat up the street with a package."

The gang of cub ballplayers in the Cigar Store asked the Night Policeman, "Who won the game? Was it the Grand Standers or the Hot Grounders took the gravvy?"

"You can search me for the answer," he told the boys. "If the snoox and the gringo come past the postoffice to-night when I sit on the front steps wondering how so many letters get lost and how so many never get answered, I will ask the snoox and the gringo and if they tell me to-night I'll tell you to-morrow night."

And ever since then when they talk ball talk in the ball towns hiding in the tall grass they

The Big Ball Game

say the only sure way to win a ball game is to have a pitcher with a spitball shirt and over that a home run shirt, both made by a snoox and a gringo.

8. Two Stories Out of Oklahoma and Nebraska.

People: Jonas Jonas Huckabuck
Mama Mama Huckabuck
Pony Pony Huckabuck

A Yellow Squash
A Silver Buckle
A Chinese Silver Slipper
    Buckle
Pop Corn

Yang Yang
Hoo Hoo
Their Mother

The Shadow of the Goose
The Left Foot of the
    Shadow of the Goose
An Oklahoma Home

The Huckabuck Family and How They Raised Pop Corn in Nebraska and Quit and Came Back

Jonas Jonas Huckabuck was a farmer in Nebraska with a wife, Mama Mama Huckabuck, and a daughter, Pony Pony Huckabuck.

"Your father gave you two names the same in front," people had said to him.

And he answered, "Yes, two names are easier to remember. If you call me by my first name Jonas and I don't hear you then

169

when you call me by my second name Jonas maybe I will.

"And," he went on, "I call my pony-face girl Pony Pony because if she doesn't hear me the first time she always does the second."

And so they lived on a farm where they raised pop corn, these three, Jonas Jonas Huckabuck, his wife, Mama Mama Huckabuck, and their pony-face daughter, Pony Pony Huckabuck.

After they harvested the crop one year they had the barns, the cribs, the sheds, the shacks, and all the cracks and corners of the farm, all filled with pop corn.

"We came out to Nebraska to raise pop corn," said Jonas Jonas, "and I guess we got nearly enough pop corn this year for the pop corn poppers and all the friends and relations of all the pop corn poppers in these United States."

And this was the year Pony Pony was going to bake her first squash pie all by herself. In

She carried the squash into the kitchen

one corner of the corn crib, all covered over with pop corn, she had a secret, a big round squash, a fat yellow squash, a rich squash all spotted with spots of gold.

She carried the squash into the kitchen, took a long sharp shining knife, and then she cut the squash in the middle till she had two big half squashes. And inside just like outside it was rich yellow spotted with spots of gold.

And there was a shine of silver. And Pony Pony wondered why silver should be in a squash. She picked and plunged with her fingers till she pulled it out.

"It's a buckle," she said, " a silver buckle, a Chinese silver slipper buckle."

She ran with it to her father and said, "Look what I found when I cut open the golden yellow squash spotted with gold spots —it is a Chinese silver slipper buckle."

"It means our luck is going to change, and we don't know whether it will be good luck

173

or bad luck," said Jonas Jonas to his daughter, Pony Pony Huckabuck.

Then she ran with it to her mother and said, "Look what I found when I cut open the yellow squash spotted with spots of gold—it is a Chinese silver slipper buckle."

"It means our luck is going to change, and we don't know whether it will be good luck or bad luck," said Mama Mama Huckabuck.

And that night a fire started in the barns, crib, sheds, shacks, cracks, and corners, where the pop corn harvest was kept. All night long the pop corn popped. In the morning the ground all around the farm house and the barn was covered with white pop corn so it looked like a heavy fall of snow.

All the next day the fire kept on and the pop corn popped till it was up to the shoulders of Pony Pony when she tried to walk from the house to the barn. And that night in all the barns, cribs, sheds, shacks, cracks and corners of the farm, the pop corn went on popping.

In the morning when Jonas Jonas Huckabuck looked out of the upstairs window he saw the pop corn popping and coming higher and higher. It was nearly up to the window. Before evening and dark of that day, Jonas Jonas Huckabuck, and his wife Mama Mama Huckabuck, and their daughter Pony Pony Huckabuck, all went away from the farm saying, "We came to Nebraska to raise pop corn, but this is too much. We will not come back till the wind blows away the pop corn. We will not come back till we get a sign and a signal."

They went to Oskaloosa, Iowa. And the next year Pony Pony Huckabuck was very proud because when she stood on the sidewalks in the street she could see her father sitting high on the seat of a coal wagon, driving two big spanking horses hitched with shining brass harness in front of the coal wagon. And though Pony Pony and Jonas Jonas were proud, very proud all that year, there never came a sign, a signal.

The next year again was a proud year, exactly as proud a year as they spent in Oskaloosa. They went to Paducah, Kentucky, to Defiance, Ohio; Peoria, Illinois; Indianapolis, Indiana; Walla Walla, Washington. And in all these places Pony Pony Huckabuck saw her father, Jonas Jonas Huckabuck, standing in rubber boots deep down in a ditch with a shining steel shovel shoveling yellow clay and black mud from down in the ditch high and high up over his shoulders. And though it was a proud year they got no sign, no signal.

The next year came. It was the proudest of all. This was the year Jonas Jonas Huckabuck and his family lived in Elgin, Illinois, and Jonas Jonas was watchman in a watch factory watching the watches.

"I know where you have been," Mama Mama Huckabuck would say of an evening to

Pony Pony Huckabuck. "You have been down to the watch factory watching your father watch the watches."

"Yes," said Pony Pony. "Yes, and this evening when I was watching father watch the watches in the watch factory, I looked over my left shoulder and I saw a policeman with a star and brass buttons and he was watching me to see if I was watching father watch the watches in the watch factory."

It was a proud year. Pony Pony saved her money. Thanksgiving came. Pony Pony said, "I am going to get a squash to make a squash pie." She hunted from one grocery to another; she kept her eyes on the farm wagons coming into Elgin with squashes.

She found what she wanted, the yellow squash spotted with gold spots. She took it home, cut it open, and saw the inside was like the outside, all rich yellow spotted with gold spots.

There was a shine like silver. She picked

and plunged with her fingers and pulled and pulled till at last she pulled out the shine of silver.

"It's a sign; it is a signal," she said. "It is a buckle, a slipper buckle, a Chinese silver slipper buckle. It is the mate to the other buckle. Our luck is going to change. Yoo hoo! Yoo hoo!"

She told her father and mother about the buckle. They went back to the farm in Nebraska. The wind by this time had been blowing and blowing for three years, and all the pop corn was blown away.

"Now we are going to be farmers again," said Jonas Jonas Huckabuck to Mama Mama Huckabuck and to Pony Pony Huckabuck. "And we are going to raise cabbages, beets and turnips; we are going to raise squash, rutabaga, pumpkins and peppers for pickling. We are going to raise wheat, oats, barley, rye. We are going to raise corn such as Indian corn and kaffir corn—but we are *not* going to raise

178

any pop corn for the pop corn poppers to be popping."

And the pony-face daughter, Pony Pony Huckabuck, was proud because she had on new black slippers, and around her ankles, holding the slippers on the left foot and the right foot, she had two buckles, silver buckles, Chinese silver slipper buckles. They were mates.

Sometimes on Thanksgiving Day and Chrismas and New Year's, she tells her friends to be careful when they open a squash.

"Squashes make your luck change good to bad and bad to good," says Pony Pony.

179

Yang Yang and Hoo Hoo, or the Song of the Left Foot of the Shadow of the Goose in Oklahoma

Yang Yang and Hoo Hoo were two girls who used to live in Battle Ax, Michigan, before they moved to Wagon Wheel Gap, Colorado, and back to Broken Doors, Ohio, and then over to Open Windows, Iowa, and at last down to Alfafa Clover, Oklahoma, where they say, "Our Oklahoma home is in Oklahoma."

One summer morning Yang Yang and Hoo

Yang Yang and Hoo Hoo, or Song of

Hoo woke up saying to each other, "Our Oklahoma home is in Oklahoma." And it was that morning the shadow of a goose flew in at the open window, just over the bed where Yang Yang and Hoo Hoo slept with their eyes shut all night and woke with their eyes open in the morning.

The shadow of the goose fluttered a while along the ceiling, flickered a while along the wall, and then after one more flutter and flicker put itself on the wall like a picture of a goose put there to look at, only it was a living picture—and it made its neck stretch in a curve and then stretch straight.

"Yang yang," cried Yang Yang. "Yang yang."

"Hoo hoo," sang Hoo Hoo. "Hoo hoo."

And while Hoo Hoo kept on calling a soft, low coaxing hoo hoo, Yang Yang kept on crying a hard, noisy nagging yang yang till everybody in the house upstairs and down and everybody in the neighbor houses heard her yang-yanging.

The shadow of the goose lifted its left wing a little, lifted its right foot a little, got up on its goose legs, and walked around and around in a circle on its goose feet. And every time it walked around in a circle it came back to the same place it started from, with its left foot or right foot in the same foot spot it started from. Then it stayed there in the same place like a picture put there to look at, only it was a living picture with its neck sometimes sticking up straight in the air and sometimes bending in a long curving bend.

Yang Yang threw the bed covers off, slid out of bed and ran downstairs yang-yanging for her mother. But Hoo Hoo sat up in bed laughing, counting her pink toes to see if there were ten pink toes the same as the morning before. And while she was counting her pink toes she looked out of the corners of her eyes at the shadow of the goose on the wall.

And again the shadow of the goose lifted its left wing a little, lifted its right foot a little, got up on its goose legs, and walked around and around in a circle on its goose feet. And every time it walked around in a circle it came back to the same place it started from, with its left foot or right foot back in the same foot spot it started from. Then it stayed there in the same place where it put itself on the wall like a picture to look at, only it was a living picture with its neck sticking up straight in the air and then changing so its neck was bending in a long curving bend.

And all the time little Hoo Hoo was sitting up in bed counting her pink toes and looking out of the corners of her eyes at the shadow of the goose.

By and by little Hoo Hoo said, "Good morning—hoo hoo for you—and hoo hoo again, I was looking at the window when you came in. I saw you put yourself on the wall like a picture. I saw you begin to walk and come back where you started from with your neck sticking straight up and your neck bending in a bend. I give you good morning. I blow a hoo hoo to you. I blow two of a hoo hoo to you."

Then the shadow of a goose, as if to answer good morning, and as if to answer what Hoo Hoo meant by saying, "I blow two of a hoo hoo to you," stretched its neck sticking up straight and long, longer than any time yet, and then bended its neck in more of a bend than any time yet.

And all the time Hoo Hoo was sitting in bed feeling of her toes with her fingers to see if she had one toe for every finger, and to see if she had one pink little toe to match her one pink little finger, and to see if she had one fat flat big toe to match her one fat flat thumb.

Then when the room was all quiet the shadow of the goose lifted its left foot and began singing—singing just as the shadow of a goose always sings—with the left foot—very

185

softly with the left foot—so softly you must listen with the softest little listeners you have deep inside your ears.

And this was the song, this was the old-time, old-fashioned left foot song the shadow of the goose sang for Hoo Hoo:

Be a yang yang if you want to.
Be a hoo hoo if you want to.

The yang yangs always yang in the morning.
The hoo hoos always hoo in the morning.

Early in the morning the putters sit putting,
Putting on your nose, putting on your ears,
Putting in your eyes and the lashes on your eyes,
Putting on the chins of your chinny chin chins.

And after singing the left foot song the shadow of the goose walked around in a long circle, came back where it started from, stopped and stood still with the proud stand-still of a goose, and then stretched its neck sticking up straight and long, longer than any time yet, and then bended its neck bent and

186

twisted in longer bends than any time yet.

Then the shadow took itself off the wall, fluttered and flickered along the ceiling and over the bed, flew out of the window and was gone, leaving Hoo Hoo all alone sitting up in bed counting her pink toes.

Out of the corners of her eyes she looked up at the wall of the room, at the place where the shadow of the goose put itself like a picture. And there she saw a shadow spot. She looked and saw it was a left foot, the same left foot that had been singing the left foot song.

Soon Yang Yang came yang-yanging into the room holding to her mother's apron. Hoo Hoo told her mother all the happenings that happened. The mother wouldn't believe it. Then Hoo Hoo pointed up to the wall, to the left foot, the shadow spot left behind by the shadow of the goose when it took itself off the wall.

And now when Yang Yang and Hoo Hoo sleep all night with their eyes shut and wake

Yang Yang and Hoo Hoo

up in the morning with their eyes open, sometimes they say, "Our Oklahoma home is in
Oklahoma," and sometimes they sing:

Be a yang yang and yang yang if you want to.
Be a hoo hoo and hoo hoo if you want to.

9. One Story About Big People Now and Little People Long Ago.

People: Peter Potato Blossom Wishes
Three Whispering Cats
Hannah
Hannah More
Susquehannah

Hoom Slimmer

How a Skyscraper and a Railroad Train Got Picked Up and Carried Away from Pig's Eye Valley Far in the Pickax Mountains

Peter Potato Blossom Wishes sat with her three cats, Hannah, Hannah More, and Susquehannah, one spring morning.

She was asking different kinds of questions of the three cats. But she always got the same answers no matter what she asked them.

They were whispering cats. Hannah was a yes-yes cat and always whispered yes-yes and nothing else. Hannah More was a no-no cat and always whispered no-no and nothing else. And Susquehannah was a stuttering cat and

How a Skyscraper and a Railroad Train
whispered halfway between yes and no, always
hesitating and nothing else.

"The bye-low is whistling his bye-low and
bye-low again," Peter said to herself with a
murmur. "It is spring in the tall timbers and
over the soft black lands. The hoo hoo and
the biddywiddies come north to make a home
again. The booblow blossoms put their cool
white lips out into the blue mist. Every way
I point my ears there is a bye-low whistling his
bye-low and bye-low again. The spring in the
timbers and black lands calls to the spring
aching in my heart."

Now the three whispering cats heard what
Peter Potato Blossom Wishes was murmuring
to herself about the spring heartache.

And Hannah, the yes-yes cat, answered yes-
yes. Hannah More, the no-no cat, answered
no-no. And Susquehannah, the stuttering cat,
hesitated halfway between yes-yes and no-no.

And Peter rubbed their fur the right way,
scratched them softly between the ears, and

murmured to herself, "It is a don't-care morning—I don't care."

And that morning her heart gave a hoist and a hist when she saw a speck of a blackbird spot far and high in the sky. Coming nearer it hummed, zoomed, hong whonged . . . shut off the hong whong . . . stoplocked and droplocked . . . and came down on the ground like a big easy bird with big wings stopped.

Hoom Slimmer slid out, wiped his hands on the oil rags, put a smear of axle grease on Peter's chin, kissed her on the nose, patted her ears two pats—and then they went into the house and had a late breakfast which was her second breakfast and his first.

"I flew till I came to Pig's Eye Valley in the Pickax Mountains," Hoom Slimmer told her. "The pickax pigs there run digging with their pickax feet and their pickax snouts. They are lean, long-legged pigs with pockets all over, fat pocket ears ahead and fat pocket tails behind, and the pockets full of rusty dust. They dip their noses in their pockets, sniff their noses full of rusty dust, and sneeze the rusty dust in each other's wrinkly, wriggly, wraggly faces.

"I took out a buzz shovel and scraper, pushed on the buzzer, and watched it dig and scrape out a city. The houses came to my ankles. The factories came to my knees. The top of the roof of the highest skyscraper came up to my nose.

"A spider ran out of a cellar. A book fell out of his mouth. It broke into rusty dust when I took hold of it. One page I saved. The reading on it said millions of people had read the book and millions more would read it."

Hoom Slimmer reached into a pocket. He took out in his hand a railroad train with an engine hooked on ahead, and a smoking car, coaches and sleeping cars hooked on behind.

"I cleaned it nice for you, Peter," he said.

"But the pickax pigs sneezed rusty dust on it. Put it in your handkerchief."

"And now," he went on, "I will wrap off the wrappers on the skyscraper. . . . Look at it! . . . It is thirty stories high. On top is a flagpole for a flag to go up. Halfway down is a clock, with the hands gone. On the first floor is a restaurant with signs, 'Watch Your Hats and Overcoats.' Here is the office of the building, with a sign on the wall, 'Be Brief.' Here the elevators ran up and down in a hurry. On doors are signs, bankers, doctors, lawyers, life insurance, fire insurance, steam hoist and operating engineers, bridge and structural iron and steel construction engineers, stocks, bonds, securities, architects, writers, detectives, window cleaners, jewelry, diamonds, cloaks, suits, shirts, sox, silk, wool, cotton, lumber, brick, sand, corn, oats, wheat, paper, ink, pencils, knives, guns, land, oil, coal, one door with a big sign, 'We Buy and Sell Anything,' another door, 'We Fix Anything,' and

195

more doors, 'None Such,' 'The World's Finest,' 'The Best in the World,' 'Oldest Establishment in the World,' 'The World's Greatest,' 'None Greater,' 'Greatest in the World,' 'Greatest Ever Known.' "

And Hoom Slimmer put his arms around the skyscraper, lifted it on his shoulder, and carried it upstairs where Peter Potato Blossom said to put it, in a corner of her sleeping room. And she took out of her handkerchief the railroad train with the engine hooked on ahead and the smoking car, coaches and sleeping cars, hooked on behind. And she put the railroad train just next to the bottom floor of the skyscraper so people on the train could step off the train and step right into the skyscraper.

"Little railroad trains and little skyscrapers are just as big for little people as big railroad trains and big skyscrapers are for big people —is it not such?" she asked Hoom Slimmer.

And for an answer he gave her a looking glass half as long as her little finger and said,

Got Picked Up and Carried Away

"The women in that skyscraper used to look at themselves from head to foot in that looking glass."

Then Peter sang out like a spring bird song, "Now we are going to forget the pickax pigs sneezing rusty dust, and the Pig's Eye Valley and the Pickax Mountains. We are going out where the bye-low is whistling his bye-low and bye-low again, where it is spring in the tall timbers and over the soft black lands, where the hoo hoo and the biddywiddies come north to make a home again and the booblow blossoms put their cool white lips out into the blue mist."

And they sat under a tree where the early green of spring crooned in the black branches, and they could hear Hannah, Hannah More and Susquehannah, whispering yes-yes, no-no, and a hesitating stutter halfway between yes-yes, and no-no, always hesitating.

10. Three Stories About the Letter X and How It Got into the Alphabet.

> *People:* An Oyster King
> Shovel Ears
> Pig Wisps
> The Men Who Change
> the Alphabets
>
> A River Lumber King
> Kiss Me
> Flax Eyes
> Wildcats
>
> A Rich Man
> Blue Silver
> Her Playmates, Singing

There are six hundred different stories told in the Rootabaga Country about the first time the letter X got into the alphabet and how and why it was. The author has chosen three (3) of the shortest and strangest of those stories and they are told in the next and following pages.

Pig Wisps

There was an oyster king far in the south who knew how to open oysters and pick out the pearls.

He grew rich and all kinds of money came rolling in on him because he was a great oyster opener and knew how to pick out the pearls.

The son of this oyster king was named Shovel Ears. And it was hard for him to remember.

"He knows how to open oysters but he forgets to pick out the pearls," said the father of Shovel Ears.

Pig Wisps

"He is learning to remember worse and worse and to forget better and better," said the father of Shovel Ears.

Now in that same place far in the south was a little girl with two braids of hair twisted down her back and a face saying, "Here we come—where from?"

And her mother called her Pig Wisps.

Twice a week Pig Wisps ran to the butcher shop for a soup bone. Before starting she crossed her fingers and then the whole way to the butcher shop kept her fingers crossed.

If she met any playmates and they asked her to stop and play crosstag or jackstones or all-around-the-mulberry-bush or the-green-grass-grew-all-around or drop-the-handkerchief, she told them, "My fingers are crossed and I am running to the butcher shop for a soup bone."

One morning running to the butcher shop she bumped into a big queer boy and bumped him flat on the sidewalk.

Pig Wisps

"Did you look where you were running?" she asked him.

"I forgot again," said Shovel Ears. "I remember worse and worse. I forget better and better."

"Cross your fingers like this," said Pig Wisps, showing him how.

He ran to the butcher shop with her, watching her keep her fingers crossed till the butcher gave her the soup bone.

"After I get it then the soup bone reminds me to go home with it," she told him. "But until I get the soup bone I keep my fingers crossed."

Shovel Ears went to his father and began helping his father open oysters. And Shovel Ears kept his fingers crossed to remind him to pick out the pearls.

He picked a hundred buckets of pearls the first day and brought his father the longest slippery, shining rope of pearls ever seen in that oyster country.

Pig Wisps

"How do you do it?" his father asked.

"It is the crossed fingers—like this," said Shovel Ears, crossing his fingers like the letter X. "This is the way to remember better and forget worse."

It was then the oyster king went and told the men who change the alphabets just what happened.

When the men who change the alphabets heard just what happened, they decided to put in a new letter, the letter X, near the end of the alphabet, the sign of the crossed fingers.

On the wedding day of Pig Wisps and Shovel Ears, the men who change the alphabets all came to the wedding, with their fingers crossed.

Pig Wisps and Shovel Ears stood up to be married. They crossed their fingers. They told each other other they would remember their promises.

Pig Wisps

And Pig Wisps had two ropes of pearls twisted down her back and a sweet young face saying, "Here we come—where from?"

Kiss Me

Many years ago when pigs climbed chimneys and chased cats up into the trees, away back, so they say, there was a lumber king who lived in a river city with many wildcats in the timbers near by.

And the lumber king said, "I am losing my hair and my teeth and I am tired of many things; my only joy is a daughter who is a dancing shaft of light on the ax handles of morning."

She was quick and wild, the lumber king's daughter. She had never kissed. Not her mother nor father nor any sweetheart ever had

Kiss Me

a love print from her lips. Proud she was. They called her Kiss Me.

She didn't like that name, Kiss Me. They never called her that when she was listening. If she happened to be listening they called her Find Me, Lose Me, Get Me. They never mentioned kisses because they knew she would run away and be what her father called her, "a dancing shaft of light on the ax handles of morning."

But—when she was not listening they asked, "Where is Kiss Me to-day?" Or they would say, "Every morning Kiss Me gets more beautiful—I wonder if she will ever in her young life get a kiss from a man good enough to kiss her."

One day Kiss Me was lost. She went out on a horse with a gun to hunt wildcats in the timbers near by. Since the day before, she was gone. All night she was out in a snowstorm with a horse and a gun hunting wild-

Out into the snowstorm Flax Eyes rode that day

cats. And the storm of the blowing snow was coming worse on the second day.

It was then the lumber king called in a long, loose, young man with a leather face and hay in his hair. And the king said, "Flax Eyes, you are the laziest careless man in the river lumber country—go out in the snowstorm now, among the wildcats, where Kiss Me is fighting for her life—and save her."

"I am the hero. I am the man who knows how. I am the man who has been waiting for this chance," said Flax Eyes.

On a horse, with a gun, out into the snowstorm Flax Eyes rode that day. Far, far away he rode to where Kiss Me, the quick wild Kiss Me, was standing with her back against a big rock fighting off the wildcats.

In that country the snowstorms make the wildcats wilder—and Kiss Me was tired of shooting wildcats, tired of fighting in the snow, nearly ready to give up and let the wildcats have her.

Kiss Me

Then Flax Eyes came. The wildcats jumped at him, and he threw them off. More wildcats came, jumping straight at his face. He took hold of those wildcats by the necks and threw them over the big rock, up into the trees, away into the snow and the wind.

At last he took all the wildcats one by one and threw them so far they couldn't come back. He put Kiss Me on her horse, rode back to the lumber king and said lazy and careless, "This is us."

The lumber king saw the face of Flax Eyes was all covered with cross marks like the letter X. And the lumber king saw the wildcats had torn the shirt off Flax Eyes and on the skin of his chest, shoulders, arms, were the cross marks of the wildcats' claws, cross marks like the letter X.

So the king went to the men who change the alphabets and they put the cross marks of the wildcats' claws, for a new letter, the letter

Kiss Me

X, near the end of the alphabet. And at the wedding of Kiss Me and Flax Eyes, the men who change the alphabets came with wildcat claws crossed like the letter X.

Blue Silver

Long ago when the years were dark and the black rains used to come with strong winds and blow the front porches off houses, and pick chimneys off houses, and blow them onto other houses, long ago when people had understanding about rain and wind, there was a rich man with a daughter he loved better than anything else in the world.

And one night when the black rain came with a strong wind blowing off front porches and picking off chimneys, the daughter of the rich man fell asleep into a deep sleep.

In the morning they couldn't wake her.

Blue Silver

The black rain with the strong wind kept up all that day while she kept on sleeping in a deep sleep.

Men and women with music and flowers came in, boys and girls, her playmates, came in—singing songs and calling her name. And she went on sleeping.

All the time her arms were crossed on her breast, the left arm crossing the right arm like a letter X.

Two days more, five days, six, seven days went by—and all the time the black rain with a strong wind blowing—and the daughter of the rich man never woke up to listen to the music nor to smell the flowers nor to hear her playmates singing songs and calling her name.

She stayed sleeping in a deep sleep—with her arms crossed on her breast—the left arm crossing the right arm like a letter X.

So they made a long silver box, just long enough to reach from her head to her feet.

And they put on her a blue silver dress and

a blue silver band around her forehead and blue silver shoes on her feet.

There were soft blue silk and silver sleeves to cover her left arm and her right arm—the two arms crossed on her breast like the letter X.

They took the silver box and carried it to a corner of the garden where she used to go to look at blue lilacs and climbing blue morning glories in patches of silver lights.

Among the old leaves of blue lilacs and morning glories they dug a place for the silver box to be laid in.

And men and women with music and flowers stood by the silver box, and her old playmates, singing songs she used to sing—and calling her name.

When it was all over and they all went away they remembered one thing most of all.

And that was her arms in the soft silk and blue silver sleeves, the left arm crossing over the right arm like the letter X.

Blue Silver

Somebody went to the king of the country and told him how it all happened, how the black rains with a strong wind came, the deep sleep, the singing playmates, the silver box— and the soft silk and blue silver sleeves on the left arm crossing the right arm like the letter X.

Before that there never was a letter X in the alphabet. It was then the king said, "We shall put the crossed arms in the alphabet; we shall have a new letter called X, so everybody will understand a funeral is beautiful if there are young singing playmates."